Into the Night

THE SAMANTHA WALSH STORY

Into the Night

THE SAMANTHA WALSH STORY

Gordon Walsh

Flanker Press Ltd.
St. John's, Newfoundland
2002

National Library of Canada Cataloguing in Publication Data

Walsh, Gordon, 1941-
    Into the night : the Samantha Walsh story / Gordon Walsh.

ISBN 1-894463-28-5

    1. Walsh, Samantha, 1986-2000. 2. Murder--Newfoundland and
    Labrador--Fleur de Lys. 3. Fleur de Lys (Nfld.)--History. I. Title.

HV6535.C32N49 2002   364.15'23'092   C2002-904243-7

PRINTED IN CANADA BY ROBINSON-BLACKMORE

First printing September 2002
Second printing September 2002

— FLANKER PRESS LTD. —

P O Box 2522, Stn C,
St. John's, Newfoundland, Canada, A1C 6K1

Toll Free: 1-866-739-4420   Telephone: (709) 739-4477
Facsimile: (709) 739-4420   E-mail: info@flankerpress.com
www.flankerpress.com

Acknowledgements

I would like to thank George and Millie Walsh for putting their faith in me to do this story about their daughter Samantha.

I would like to say a special thank you to my wife Clotilda and daughter Joy for their help, also my daughters Helena, Roberta, Kristie, and my son Gordon. To those who did the photocopying and offered the use of their newspaper clippings and photographs, thanks.

Thanks go to authors Carmelita McGrath for suggesting the title *Into the Night*, Tom Moore for referring me to Flanker Press, and Kenneth Young for reading the manuscript. At Flanker Press, thanks to editor Jerry Cranford, Margo Cranford, Vera McDonald, and publisher Garry Cranford.

Thanks go to Maura Hanrahan for writing the foreword to the book and to Paul Butler who edited the book by long-distance from Ottawa.

Foreword

A few days after the lifeless body of thirteen-year-old Samantha Walsh was found, reporter Ryan Cleary wrote in the *Telegram*: "the Baie Verte Peninsula, like every other nook and cranny of the province, cries out in distress over the loss of Sammy B."

Cleary was not exaggerating or being sentimental; this was the truth.

I was in St. Anthony Airport on my way to coastal Labrador when word spread through the lounge that the missing girl from Fleur de Lys had been found dead. The airport terminus was eerily quiet. Such a grim discovery was expected—Sam had been gone for eighteen long, cold winter days—but everyone who heard the news was grief-stricken. People silently shed tears or tried to hold them back.

Eventually I flew farther north into the Metis community of Black Tickle to find that the high-school stu-

dents there had written a letter of sympathy to
Samantha's friends in Fleur de Lys. As I travelled, I made
the same discovery as author Gordon Walsh as he went
back and forth over the province's roads: that ours was a
collective grief.

This might seem odd, though, as most of us had not
heard of Samantha until she went missing that Sunday
night. Nor were her parents well known. Like hundreds
of other outports, Samantha's home community was a
quiet little place you did not hear much about. And she
was not the first Newfoundland child to disappear in this
manner; just before Christmas in 1981, fourteen-year-old
Dana Bradley was abducted and murdered in St. John's,
the capital city. Newfoundlanders still remember Dana's
name. We'll never forget Sam's either.

Samantha Bertha Walsh was born on May 27, 1986—
in Newfoundland. Her mother Millie Lewis Walsh was
nine months pregnant and living in Fort McMurray,
Alberta, when her husband George bundled his family
into their truck and headed straight for home. George
was determined that his baby would be born a
Newfoundlander. And she was.

Samantha was a proud Newfoundlander, too. In her
haunting rendition of *Saltwater Joys* (renamed
Samantha's Song after her death) she sings, "I was born
down by the water and it's here I'm going to stay, I've
searched for all the reasons why I should go away..."

Samantha was only five when the groundfish moratorium brought a centuries-old way of life to a halt. With no viable future in sight, thousands of families closed their homes forever and drove off to the mainland. Some of them were Sam's neighbours on the Baie Verte Peninsula. Listening to Samantha sing, you sense that she's considered all the turmoil into which her island had been thrown. And she's chosen to respond with stubbornness and determination in spite of that. After all, she was George's daughter.

Then as Samantha's picture flashed on the Newfoundland television news every night, she became everyone's daughter. We grew familiar with the little round clips that held her brown hair to the side of her head, the big grin, the bright eyes, the baby fat she still carried on her cheeks. We didn't know a lot about her, though, only that she was missing and that, as the days went by unchanging, an entire community was being driven mad with frustration and grief. These people, the people of Fleur de Lys, were coping with the apparent loss of one of their children in what seemed to be the most heinous way. For them, this was the most awful in-your-face nightmare. And it was so unexpected.

Fleur de Lys is the most northerly community on the Baie Verte Peninsula on Newfoundland's northeast coast. It has a long-standing association with French fishermen who named it after a large rock in the harbour that reminded them of their national flower, the fleur-de-lys or lily. Petit Nord, a rich fishing ground, was nearby, and it kept the French coming back to this area year after year. Once part of the French Shore, Fleur de Lys welcomed French fishermen long after their presence had diminished elsewhere on the coast. For many years, the community was an important stopover for vessels en route to Labrador or France.

According to the region's oral history, the first settlers were Michael and Robert Walsh. The 1857 census reports that there were thirty people living in Fleur de Lys, all Roman Catholic. Some of the early settlers could speak French, and relations between the two ethnic groups were generally smooth. Tradition also says, though, that the settlers moved their boats and nets from certain fishing grounds in response to threats from the seasonal French fishermen. However they managed it, overt conflict was avoided—as it was many years later as the community coped with a missing child and suspicions that one among them was guilty.

Samantha's forebears, the Walshes, were of Irish descent. By 1869, they were neighbours to the Lewises, believed to be of French origins (their original name may be Louis). This is Samantha's mother's family. Shortly after the Lewises arrived, the first school was built. It's not known if the Lewises were the driving force behind the school, but their descendant Millie became a teacher.

The community grew and grew. The sixty-five families who called Fleur de Lys home in 1911 fished cod, salmon and herring, and hunted seals. Later they worked in the lumber industry and in mining in nearby Baie Verte. Eventually there were more miners than fishermen in town. Fleur de Lys became a receiving community for some of those outport Newfoundlanders forced to move to bigger settlements as a result of the federal and provincial governments' controversial resettlement programs. Almost seven hundred people lived in Fleur de Lys as the program drew to a close. This was the largest the community would ever be.

Fleur de Lys was home for George and Millie Walsh; this was the place their roots lay. They were thrilled to be raising Samantha and her older brother Sandy there. Soon after they moved back to the community, they built a large home on a bluff above the harbour. When George went to buy the lumber to build the house, he brought toddler Sam with him. While he was talking to the sawmill operator, he left Sam in the truck, next to the envelope of cash on the front seat. But there was no money left when George returned to the truck: Sam had opened the envelope and thrown the bills out the window, where the winds carried them away.

Samantha, of course, was forgiven. In her short life, this child knew only love.

She was crazy about sports, especially soccer, and even more passionate about music. She was a Céline Dion fan; her favourite song was *My Heart Will Go On* from the film *Titanic*. She loved Newfoundland music, too: she spent part of her last day alive singing Ennis Sisters and Fables songs with her dad as he drove to a local ski run.

Not long after that, the horror started. In this book, Gordon Walsh brings us inside the heart of someone who is living with the knowledge that a child they love is missing and probably murdered. Gordon makes us feel a gamut of emotions: fear, vengeance, sorrow, hope, and love. His honesty is compelling; he is forthright about how he feels and unconcerned about whether or not anyone will judge him for his feelings. He takes us into the very minute when George and Millie realize something is wrong, when the men and women of the community debate what to do, when he sits in the church near the young man who was later found guilty of killing his niece. This is not a book from which the reader can experience any sense of detachment.

I think this will be particularly true of Newfoundland readers. By the time Samantha died, we had lost so many of our young people. The demise of the cod-fishery pushed our children and youth and their parents to mainland towns where they would always be strangers. For the first time, a generation of Newfoundlanders would not start their working lives in fishing boats. Indeed, they would never even see boats unload steak cod, or have the stench of cod guts invade their nostrils. The inshore cod-fishery that was the backbone of Newfoundland ended, and we were left with only a plaque to commemorate it. The rural communities that were the backbone of Newfoundland were (and are) under threat in a way they never were before. For us, the 1990s were largely about loss, a loss sometimes too big to face.

Samantha's death meant a continuation of that loss. Especially because of her innocence and that of her community. Rural Newfoundland was economically depressed after the moratorium, but it was safe, we assumed. Then the girl with the little round clips disappeared. Even worse, another of our children was responsible for her disappearance. Still a child, Samantha was subjected to the kind of violence against women that we associate with American movies and television. But it is our problem, too. Suddenly we felt safe no more.

In spite of this, the story of Samantha's loss and the search for her little body gives us much reason for hope. This is a tale of a community coping and coming together in enlightened and even sophisticated ways. Readers from outside Newfoundland will marvel at how it is natural for Gordon to visit the parents of the youth who murdered Samantha to empathize with their pain. They will be startled to see how the youth's parents visit

George and Millie to convey their sympathy—and are welcomed by the Walshes. Most heartening is the fact that none of this is done in a self-conscious or self-righteous manner; it is a natural and enduring expression of rural Newfoundland culture.

Readers may also wonder at the Fleur de Lys men's hesitance to ask the young man's parents to pressure him to take a polygraph (or "lie detector") test. Everyone is convinced of his guilt. With their own hands tied because of rules and regulations, the police want them to do this. Gordon and the others eventually agree to talk to the boy's parents, but then they keep postponing it. They are skilled in conflict avoidance; their history is one of people working together in a relatively harsh geophysical environment. Their skills are in empathy and cooperation, not in doing things that would divide an already dividing community. This is one of the things about rural Newfoundland that is well worth saving.

Yet, for all that, this story is a sad one. It is pain-filled, ugly, and maddening. It's one of those stories in which you know what's going to happen but you keep hoping it will turn out for the best anyway. It doesn't, of course, and the sad truth is that there can be no closure for Samantha's family. A piece of them is gone and always will be. Nor will the pain ever leave the family of the young man who committed this crime against Samantha.

Someday we might be able to take heart in the words of the priest at Samantha's funeral. He asked the young of Fleur de Lys to plant flowers and seeds of compassion and forgiveness. He asked the adults to uproot all the seeds of anger. "This little girl would not want (to leave) a legacy of bitterness or a trail of ugliness," he said. He was right; Samantha, this child of rural Newfoundland, deserved much better than that.

Maura Hanrahan,
July 13, 2002

For Sam

Prologue

Sometimes I think of Sam in happier times, like Christmas Eve of 1999, when she was at my home. It was a tradition for most of the family to come to my house for Christmas supper. This year, George, Millie and Sam were able to make it. We shook hands, wished each other a Merry Christmas, and exchanged small gifts. We then sat at the table to have supper before attending Christmas Mass.

I could tell Sam was very excited about the holiday season. She looked beautiful in her floor-length grey skirt and pretty red top. I wondered what plans she had for the years to come, but I didn't ask her. I guessed she was thinking about the things she would do.

Sam liked music from the very beginning. I had heard her sing when she was very young, so small I thought she wouldn't be able to remember all the words. In 1996, Fleur de Lys had held a reunion, a come-home-year celebration. It was headed and organized by Sam's mother and father, and the event promised to be a huge success. Although Sam was young, she was very interested in what was going to take place that August.

There were plenty of games and activities at the soiree, and of course music. People came from all over for the event and brought their kids with them. Some were Sam's friends, others relatives, and some she had never seen before. That didn't make a difference, since she was the kind of person who made friends easily.

Music was the part that interested Sam the most. She loved music. Some of the top local bands showed for the reunion. There must have been half a dozen or more that played, and Sam enjoyed every one. She would go up to the musicians when they weren't on stage and talk with them. She wasn't a bold girl, nor was she particularly shy; she was simply curious. If she wanted to know something, she would simply ask.

In preparation for the come-home-year celebrations, we had agreed to release a tape of songs. We called it "The Children of Fleur de Lys." All who wished to sing were given the chance, old and young alike. On that tape can be heard the very young, sweet, clear voice of Samantha Walsh singing the song she loved best, *Saltwater Joys*.

I always thought she might have a chance in the music industry. That would be a great thing, if that's what she wanted to do in life. But I was certain of one thing: she was growing into a beautiful young woman. I told her this, and she smiled at me.

"Thanks," she said.

Sam would never see another Christmas.

Chapter 1

"Gord," called a familiar voice from the open window. It was Millie, my sister-in-law. I could tell right away from her tone that something was wrong.

Sunday, February 6, 2000 was a beautiful, crisp winter day. People went about their business just as on any other Sunday, some going to church, more driving their Ski-Doos, others taking walks. Some just stayed home and relaxed. The kids, as usual, were heading out for a day of fun. Sam and her dad headed out to Baie Verte so she could have a day skiing with her friends at Copper Creek Mountain.

Later in the evening, I went on my nightly walk. I left my house at the usual time, between ten and ten-thirty. As I walked with the moon and stars shining above, the wind began to bite through my clothes. This evening had to be the coldest in the last couple of winters. I wished I had put on my heavy winter parka.

I met others on their own evening walks and exchanged greetings with a casual "Hi" or "Good night." In our community, it was very rare for people not to speak, since we all knew each other and most are related in some way.

As I continued walking, I thought of the little town in which my family and I had lived for so long. I thought of how lucky we were to live in a small place where I could go out on the street at any time of the day or night, where I could let my kids do the same and feel assured of their safety. I had visited many big cities, like Toronto, Montreal, Edmonton, and Calgary, where people lived in high-rise apartment buildings. It seemed to me that those poor kids were being raised in jail. In Fleur de Lys I could walk out my front door and step onto my front lawn. I didn't have to get into an elevator and go up or down eight, ten, or fifteen floors just to get in or out of my home. In Toronto, people keep their doors locked day and night. Right here in this little town of Fleur de Lys we let our children roam wherever they wanted. There was no reason to lock the doors at night, and certainly not during the day.

I finally reached the point where I usually turned toward home. It seemed to be getting even colder. My thoughts shifted from the comfort and safety of our little town to the cozy and comforting heat of my wood stove. I didn't meet any more walkers and assumed the cold must be keeping them home.

I saw two cars pull out of the parking lot of Skipper Shea's Lounge. One of them I didn't recognize, and this one pulled over across the street from me. I peered at the darkened window but couldn't make out the people inside.

"Gord," called a familiar voice from the open window. It was Millie, my sister-in-law. I could tell right away from her tone that something was wrong.

As I approached the car, Millie asked if I had seen anyone on my walk. George, my brother, was sitting beside her. I told her that I hadn't. Then George asked if I had seen Sam anywhere.

There have been a few times in my life when people have gone missing for short periods of time. But I cannot fully explain the feeling I had when my brother asked me this. Here were George and Millie, out at this hour and close to panic, asking me if I had seen their daughter. Last I had heard, Sam had gone skiing for the day, but I hadn't seen her since.

"I wonder if Sam is at Charlie's house," Millie offered. Sam and her cousin Charlie Walsh sometimes did their homework together. Without hesitation, I assured George and Millie I would go to Charlie's house and ask if he had seen Sam.

It turned out that she had not been there for a few days. From there I went directly home to tell my wife, Clotilda, and my daughter, Kristie that Sam was missing. I asked Kristie to phone her friends and find out if any of them had seen her cousin.

I left the house again to check on George and Millie, realizing as I stepped outside how cold the night had gotten. It occurred to me that Sam may have gotten on a snowmobile with one of her friends, gone on a trail up in the country and broken down. On a night like this, I feared, they could surely freeze to death.

When I arrived at George's place, my fear for Sam was bordering on panic. Once inside and out of the cold, I could still feel my hands shaking. I found it very hard to speak, but thinking of Sam freezing out in the woods somewhere got me talking. Slowly and deliberately, I forced myself to tell George and Millie about the possibility of Sam being stranded by a broken-down Ski-Doo.

I said we should get our own Ski-Doos and begin a search of all the known trails. It was a good idea, they said, and before we left, George asked Millie to call the police and the local fire brigade. From that very moment, the search was on. On my way to the door, I glanced uncomfortably at George and Millie and saw that they were both in tears. I looked at the clock on the wall. It was 11:00 P.M.

First I went to the home of my friend, Andy Stuckless. Andy owned a Ski-Doo, and I knew he wouldn't mind being called out of bed to go out looking for Sam and whoever might be with her. He roused himself at the sound of my banging on his door, realizing something was wrong. We didn't waste any time, and we talked while Andy dressed for the cold. He asked me if Sam had ever stayed out late before and I told him she hadn't.

We both agreed that instead of checking the Ski-Doo trails we should first check along the edge of the harbour ice and also investigate the surrounding wharves. But before we went our separate ways, I told Andy that everyone would be gathering at the town hall to organize the search.

I started for home. By this time, everyone in Fleur de Lys was on the move. Those who had been in bed asleep were wide awake and roaming the streets. Ski-Doos were revving up and heading for the town hall. I didn't go to the hall with Andy because I wanted to see if Clo or Kristie had learned anything from the phone calls they had made. A part of me was expecting good news, but deep down I was terrified that there would be no news at all. When I walked in, their expressions confirmed my fears. They had called all of Sam's friends, but no one had seen her.

I peered through the window and across the street at the town hall. A large crowd had already gathered, and no one seemed to mind the temperature, which was now minus twenty-five degrees Celsius. Seeing there was nothing else that could be done at home, we walked across the street and joined the others at the hall. Not surprisingly, most of Fleur de Lys was in attendance.

The town hall was filled to capacity with anxious onlookers as the local fire brigade made plans for the search. Tom Walsh, our acting fire chief, caught sight of me and called me over. "This is a predicament we don't find ourselves in very often," he said. "We're not experienced in this kind of thing." He asked if I had any ideas.

I didn't think Sam was in anyone's house, or at least not where anybody was living now. Tom decided that we should search the town again. He instructed us to search everything: knock on every door, go in every shed, every cellar, check all cars, trucks, garbage boxes, under buildings, under patios, and walk around every standing structure. We were to check all fishing wharves, as Andy and I had discussed earlier, and every place a person could hide or be hidden. We were organized into groups of two or three and sent out to different areas of the town. It was now a quarter past midnight, and bitterly cold.

My wife Clo and I searched our assigned location and left only when we were absolutely certain that Sam was not there. We returned to the town hall to report our findings. Time passed, and the searchers returned one after another. Their expressions told us in advance what their reports were. Some looked sad, others scared, but every face told the same story. Sam was nowhere to be found.

The last time anyone had seen her was when she left her grandmother Walsh's house at six-thirty that evening. She had been on her way home to do her homework for school. When she first arrived at her grandmother's house, she had removed all her winter clothing before sitting down for supper, but when she left for home, she had left behind her ski pants and gloves. Now all Sam was wearing were her jacket, her cap, and her PJ bottoms.

Seven hours had passed, and I feared that Sam had frozen to death if that was all she was wearing. I didn't dare say anything, not with George and Millie standing close by. I was agonizing over this when the last of the search parties came through the door with some news. They had been talking to a young boy who said he had seen Sam on the ice at a place called the Little Bottom. The boy said that he and a couple of friends were copying there—jumping from one floating ice pan to another—when a young man came along on a three-wheel all terrain vehicle.

Shortly after, Sam came along, and the boys saw her get on the ATV and drive away with the young man. It was something, but this bit of news did nothing to put my fears to rest. The young man Sam had supposedly driven away with was here now, in the hall, eating sandwiches and drinking coffee.

When Michael Lewis was questioned about giving Sam a ride on his ATV, he said he drove her as far as the bus shelter and dropped her off. From there he hadn't seen where she had gone, nor had he seen her since. The bus shelter across the street from George and Millie's house was Sam's last known whereabouts.

I talked it over with a couple of men back from the search. One fellow remarked that it seemed strange the young man hadn't taken Sam all the way to her house, considering she lived directly across the street from the bus shelter.

"I'm sure he doesn't mind crossing the road on his trike," he said. I knew what he meant. Michael was always on the road, day and night. He lived on that trike.

Normally, a person wasn't considered missing unless he or she had been gone for twenty-four hours or more, but the police from nearby Baie Verte were on the scene two hours after they were called. First they interviewed some of the people in the hall. Then, they took Michael to their car for questioning. He repeated his story: he had dropped Sam off at the bus shelter.

When the police returned to the hall, they suggested the town be searched again. I felt that Sam was no longer in Fleur de Lys, but I agreed anyway. It was the only thing that could be done.

Clo and I decided we would search the same area again. My daughter Kristie, her friend Charlotte Philpott, and Michael Lewis were waiting for us at the door. As we made our way to them, I overheard a police officer speak to George and Millie.

"I don't need to do this in private," I heard George respond. "We can talk right here."

"No," the policeman insisted, "we'll do it in the other room."

More police, these from the city of Corner Brook, arrived with a tracking dog. Once again the reality of the situation descended on me like a huge weight. Looking at all the police officers from Baie Verte and Corner Brook and thinking that Sam was missing for just under ten hours, I became frightened of how this day might end. The police seemed to share my thoughts. The fact that the Baie Verte police had called in their Corner Brook detachment for reinforcements confirmed it: they were taking this very seriously.

The K-9 unit went to work. The policeman took his dog from the van and went to the bus shelter. It tried to pick up a scent, anything to go on, but turned up nothing. The officer explained that there was too much activity around the shelter for the dog to pick up a scent.

The police kept coming back to Michael Lewis's story. There was something about it that didn't add up. When asked, he had told them the ATV had not stopped at the bus shelter, but drove past and went in over the hill. But he told us that he had dropped Sam off at the shelter. Did he or didn't he? Was he hiding something?

Clo and I searched every inch of the harbour, but we knew we wouldn't find anything this time either. We combed the place three times, and still no clues presented themselves as to Sam's whereabouts. We were fast losing hope, as were the others.

Chapter 2

I still couldn't help but think Sam was dead, and that now it was just a matter of finding her little body. This I could not bring myself to mention to George and Millie. It was just a raw, eating feeling in my stomach that I would have to live with.

The next day dawned a bitter minus twenty-six degrees. The Ski-Doos were lined up at the side door of the town hall, ready to go again. The search parties had scoured the trails in the dark, but it would be wise to do so again when the trails were well lit. The same went for the rest of the town.

Wherever we looked, people were searching. There wasn't a place in Fleur de Lys that wasn't searched, no door that wasn't opened. People scanned the shoreline, eyes fixed on the snow or ice for signs of life. Periodically, searchers returned to the hall to report, have a coffee, talk a bit, or just to sit and think. We felt helpless and frustrated, not knowing what to do. We searched the same places over and over again, knowing each time we wouldn't find anything, but unable to come up with any better ideas. All hope seemed to be lost when the Ski-Doo drivers began to arrive with reports the same as ours.

Fourteen hours after Sam had last been seen, more professionals arrived to plan and organize the search parties. Search and Rescue come in from Springdale, and another crew from Bishop's Falls. The investigators set up groups, each one including a local resident. Together they searched all houses and vacant buildings again, but this time inside them—in and under beds, in fridges, deep-freezes, closets, cabinets, garbage pails, attics, anywhere a person could be hidden.

Still nothing was found.

The previous day there had been a small opening in the ice near the place where Sam was last seen by the boy who was copying with his friends. But today it had frozen over after a bitterly cold night, and the police wanted that area searched as well. After breaking up the ice and scouting the outlying area, however, this lead also proved to be false.

People stayed out regardless, although it was clear they felt their efforts were in vain. I thought the answer was staring us right in the face, personally. Although the matter was best left in the capable hands of the police, I felt that Michael Lewis and his ATV were the only clues worth pursuing.

Rumours were starting. Sam had run away. She had committed suicide. Someone had abducted her.

I didn't believe that Sam, a happy, well-adjusted youngster, ever had it in her mind to run away. She had everything she wanted, as much as any other kid in Fleur de Lys. Her dad took her everywhere she wanted to go, and if he wasn't able to do it himself, he would see to it that she got to her destination. If she did commit suicide, why couldn't we find her body? The third rumour, that Sam had been abducted, was the only one I allowed myself to believe. There was a lot of gossip about a red car that had been seen at approximately 6:30 P.M. Sunday near the bus shelter, and someone else reported seeing a small red car, possibly the same one, drive through town around the same time. One person said a red car passed them at a high speed on the Baie Verte highway.

The police checked these leads, but ruled out any connection to Sam's disappearance. When people fear for the safety of a small child, when they find themselves unable to help, they start imagining things. Rumours, though unfounded, take on a life of their own. People start believing in these rumours despite themselves.

Still, during the first couple of days I did feel that Sam had been abducted by someone. I even thought it might be connected to a gold robbery the police had uncovered at the mine not far from our community. This had been big news the previous month, especially in an area where nothing much happens. I told one of the investigators of my feelings, and he agreed that it might be something worth looking into.

Although I didn't believe she had run away, I knew this explanation was the best scenario for finding Sam alive. If she had been abducted, the chances of us finding her were much slimmer. There was a second word after "abduction" running through my mind, one I could not bring myself to voice. A lot of people were thinking the same thing, but few admitted to having it in their thoughts. "Murder" was not an easy word to use at this time.

On Tuesday, February 8, the phones were ringing continuously with people calling to know if there were any signs or leads on Sam. Many wanted to know if there was anything they could do. Some had elected to call me so they could keep the line free at my brother's house. Others said they didn't want to bother George and Millie during this stressful time.

One night a lady in Corner Brook, Sandra Park, phoned me. She spoke in a very comforting tone and asked me to take good care of my brother and his wife. She added if there was anything we needed, the people of Corner Brook were ready for us. While I talked to her, I was crying, and I am sure she was crying too. As I write this, I cry again.

Another call came from a man I worked with many years ago, Clifford Rice. We talked about Sam, and he asked me to tell George that he had called. If there was anything he could do for George, he said, we shouldn't hesitate to call.

People were arriving from all the surrounding towns, eager to lend a hand to the residents of Fleur de Lys. They provided enormous moral support, as we were standing around feeling useless and lost after finding no clues leading to my missing niece. There was just one lead, I thought, although I didn't know if the police were treating it as one. My thoughts were stuck on Michael Lewis, his ATV, and the bus shelter.

A police officer came to my house to take a statement from me. When I told him everything I knew and everything I thought, we sat and drank coffee together and had a chat off the record. What he told me then took me by surprise. He said that Michael Lewis, the young man who had last seen Sam and who occupied my every waking thought these days, had refused to take a lie detector test.

"I wonder why," he said. "I don't think the young lad is shy, and I'm pretty sure he isn't afraid of anything or anyone."

The policeman looked across the table at me with a changed expression. "Mr. Walsh," he said, "I think you're right. I've been doing this job for twenty-five years, and he is the most brazen boy I have ever come in contact with."

After he left, I sat thinking—something I had been doing a lot of for the last few days and nights. At that moment I knew Sam was dead. I knew in my heart that Michael was involved. Was it an accident? I hoped her death wasn't deliberate. The word "murder" gave me the shivers.

I learned that my brother George had gone to the Baie Verte Junction on the Trans Canada Highway. A man from a nearby town had taken his daughter there to meet the bus bound for St. John's and reported that he had seen Sam sitting near the restaurant's window as he passed by. Furthermore, a second source reported a young girl matching Sam's description had been sighted there inquiring about bus fare and was accompanied by a young man. They had sat at a window in the restaurant for twenty or thirty minutes.

Another lead on top of that one had sent George to the Junction. There had been a break-and-enter at a cabin nearby, and it was discovered that somebody had slept there—maybe Sam. This fresh lead brought the media to the scene.

The lady who ran the restaurant said she was a hundred per cent sure the girl she had seen was Sam. The police passed this information on to George, and later that evening I saw my brother on the news, begging his baby to come home. My heart broke for him. Never in my life had I seen anyone in so much turmoil. Those who didn't see the news item will never know, and there is not a writer alive who can fully describe the broken man I saw standing in the freezing cold.

That night I joined George and Millie for coffee, listening more than talking. Everyone but me seemed to think Sam had been at the Junction.

"What do you think?" Jim Lewis, one of Sam's uncles, said to me. "You ain't saying much."

"I'm not so sure it was Sam they saw," I replied.

The phone rang. It was someone wanting to speak to George, someone who had been on the bus that day. The caller told George that they had seen two teenagers fitting the description of Sam and the young boy sighted in the restaurant. This seemed to make things better for George and Millie, but I wasn't convinced. I wanted to tell my brother and sister-in-law not to get their hopes up, but the memory of George on television just one hour earlier silenced me.

I still couldn't help but think Sam was dead, and that now it was just a matter of finding her little body. This I could not bring myself to mention to George and Millie. It was just a raw, eating feeling in my stomach that I would have to live with.

A psychic arrived in Fleur de Lys from St. John's. She had brought another lady with her, and the two of them went to George's house. The following day, as I drove the psychic's friend to her home in the Mi'kmaq community of Conne River, I asked what they had found. She said she was a spiritual healer and couldn't offer much help in finding Sam. She was there, she said, to help both George and Millie, and to help bring Sam back into the light and help her on her way.

"That makes two of us who think Sam is dead," I said.

She nodded. Sam had been taken to some cabin, but was not there now, she said. She felt that Sam had since been taken from the cabin and hidden.

This was my first trip to Conne River and I was surprised at the size of the place. I had pictured it to be much smaller. I dropped the lady off, and on the way back stopped for lunch by the highway. As soon as I entered the restaurant, I overheard one of the waitresses being asked if she knew whether they had found the missing girl yet. She answered that she hadn't heard anything since the night before.

I sat at a table in the middle of the restaurant and soon discovered that everyone was talking about the same thing. What happened to poor Samantha Walsh?

"What's the name of that place?" I heard one woman ask. "I keep forgetting the name."

Everywhere I went it was the same.

Chapter 3

How could a man be so calm after taking the life of someone, either by accident or on purpose? Even if he had nothing to do with it, did it not bother him that Sam's parents were asking questions as if they fully believed he was responsible? I thought I knew him well, but the way he had been acting lately seemed strange to me.

I kept my eye on Michael Lewis and his ATV. These days he was out cruising the roads more than ever. He didn't seem to mind the police presence, even though there were so many of them watching him and everyone else like a hawk. They were as puzzled as the rest of us.

The police called a meeting at the church to update the community on events. Progress was slow, but they felt sure they would solve the mystery of Sam's disappearance. They asked for any clues, even if they seemed unimportant to us, anything that could turn out to be helpful to the investigation. They told us only what they wanted us to know.

George said a few words after the police had finished their update. He thanked everyone for coming to the meeting and for all their hard work and support they were providing. He repeated the instructions given by the police a minute ago, that there may be something small, some insignificant detail we were overlooking. Little things, he concluded, could sometimes lead to big things.

I had to make a trip to Deer Lake Airport near Corner Brook to pick up my brother, John, who was coming home from Ontario. I decided to leave early so that I could visit the restaurant at Baie Verte Junction myself and talk to the lady who had supposedly spotted Sam. When I arrived I saw that I was the only customer. I ordered a coffee and approached a lady I thought could have been the one I was looking for.

"I'm sorry," she said. "It couldn't have been Sam. That same girl came back on the bus today."

I felt a sinking feeling in the pit of my stomach. George and Millie and the rest of Fleur de Lys were now back at square one. This of course didn't surprise me, but there had been a part of me hoping despite my doubts that Sam was out there somewhere.

But hope wasn't enough. This had been just one of countless false sightings of a missing person.

The search was intensifying. A helicopter with an infrared camera on board arrived. The chopper was to search the area between Fleur de Lys and the Trans Canada Highway eighty-nine kilometres away. The investigators also brought divers in to search under the ice where Sam was last seen by the group of boys. I asked one of the divers why they thought Sam was under the ice when she had been seen boarding an ATV and leaving the area. He told me they didn't expect to find anything, of course, but were given specific instructions to search and double-search. It was simply a process of elimination.

It turned out he was right—they didn't find any trace of Sam. That may have come as a relief to some of the townspeople, but not to me. The police were openly searching for signs of a body now, and that frightened me. But where was her body? We had retraced all of Sam's steps on February 6 and always come to dead ends. All leads had been pursued, except one.

George and Millie invited Michael Lewis to their house so that they could question him themselves. Had he really dropped Sam at the bus shelter across the street? Yes. Had he and Sam gone for a ride and had an accident? No. There was no need to be scared, my brother and sister-in-law reassured him. If he was involved in Sam's disappearance somehow, the best thing to do would be to tell the truth right now.

But nothing like that happened, Michael said.

Later that evening, he was seen hanging out with some of the other teenagers around the B & B Takeout. He said he was pissed off because they were trying to put the blame on him. I don't know if he realized it at the time, but at least half the people in town considered him their number one suspect. That number was growing every minute he delayed taking the lie detector test.

I thought of his behavior the first night out with the rescue party. "You don't have to look in there," he would tell Kristie and her friend Charlotte, pointing to an old shed or house. Then he would take the flashlight and search the place ahead of them anyway. But there were other nights when we would come in for a cup of hot coffee and see him sitting in the town hall eating sandwiches and looking as relaxed as a schoolboy at recess.

How could a man be so calm after taking the life of someone, either by accident or on purpose? Even if he had nothing to do with it, did it not bother him that Sam's parents were asking questions as if they fully believed he was responsible? I thought I knew him well, but the way he had been acting lately seemed strange to me.

Fleur de Lys's hopes of finding Sam were tempered only by the raw fear that all they would find would be a body, so when the chopper returned after a thorough search and with no solid leads, we experienced mixed feelings of disappointment and renewed hope. The pilot reported that the alarms on his control panel had been set off by numerous rabbits in the area, nothing else. He promised to stay as long as he was needed.

Everywhere we could think of, any place where Sam might have been hidden, was re-searched time after time. We even sent a longliner out beyond the harbour boundaries to check along the shoreline. Someone had mentioned at the town hall that Sam might have been taken out that way. But like all our other ideas, this one didn't turn up anything.

It was ruled out that someone from outside of town had abducted Sam. People were getting nervous; parents were warning their children not to get in any cars or on any Ski-Doos. Specifically, the children were ordered not to get on Michael Lewis's ATV. Many thought the police should have taken the trike at the very beginning, reasoning that it was the last vehicle on which Sam had been seen alive. But others had a theory.

"Maybe the police are letting him keep it for a reason."

At first I hadn't realized just how frightened Fleur de Lys had become. The adults were scared for their children's safety, sure, but it dawned on me that perhaps they were afraid for themselves, too. Those who hadn't usually locked their doors were doing so now, even during the day. I soon found myself doing the same.

I can best describe it as a lonesome, sickening feeling that stayed with us at all times. Throwing ourselves into our work, into searching for our little girl, did nothing to shake it. I never knew what it was like to feel so alone and terrified before, but I did now. We in Fleur de Lys weren't alone. It was a feeling shared by people across the whole province. When my friends and neighbours told me of their fears I would tell them it was normal and that people from as far away as Corner Brook and St. John's felt the same.

Over the phone, men and women told me their hearts were breaking for us. They didn't need to tell me. I could hear it in their voices.

The first week Sam was missing I made many trips to the airport to pick up brothers and sisters and other relatives of people in town. They were coming home to help family cope with the tragedy. After the first couple of trips, workers at the airport came to know me as "Samantha Walsh's uncle." They would gather around, trying to get every bit of information they could. "This is unbelievable," one of the ladies at the ticket booth said to me. "All our customers talk about is their concern for the missing girl."

The authorities were treating this case as a major crime. Everywhere I looked, police were coming and going. They went in and out of people's houses all day long. The officer who had first told me that Michael had refused the lie detector test came to my house again to get a statement from Kristie.

When he finished questioning my daughter, we sat at the kitchen table and talked while he drank his coffee. He struck me as a polite and honest man. They had twenty-seven officers on this case, he told me. These men were the best in the province, he added, highly trained and experienced in missing persons cases.

We talked about Michael Lewis. The officer said he was more convinced than ever the boy was involved in Sam's disappearance. I liked talking to this fellow, as his line of thinking was much the same as mine. He had been the first to admit I was right when I noted that something didn't add up with Michael's statement.

"Whatever happened to this young girl," the officer said, "this young boy knows. I guarantee it."

He asked me if I had been at the church service last night. The boy had been there, he said.

"I sat close to him, where I could study his face," the officer explained, "and his expression was stone cold. There were no tears, no sadness, no emotion whatso-ever. You know," he added, "I looked at all the people's faces in that church, and every person in there had tears in his eyes, including me, and I don't even know the family."

Yes, I said, I too had been at the service, and I had watched Michael. I agreed there was nothing to see in his face. No fear, no sorrow, no remorse.

The underwater team soon came back with more divers and equipment. They were going to search the entire harbour bottom for a body. Some of the townsmen stood ready to lend a helping hand. The ice was about eighteen inches thick and had to be cut with a chainsaw. The holes the divers were to work with were approximately seven by seven feet, and they were spaced to the required distances.

It was Sunday, February 13, exactly one week after Sam had disappeared. The divers spent most of the day searching. People had gathered on the fish plant's wharf, and each time a diver returned to the surface, they would hold their breath in fear of what might be found.

To the north of the diving area, on the hill I could clearly see Sam's house, with its big windows that reached from ceiling to floor. I wondered if George and Millie were home. If so, they were probably looking through those windows right now at divers searching the bottom for their baby girl.

Chapter 4

We needed answers, but there was no one to give them to us. Outside the town hall, a woman said to me that no one in Fleur de Lys was safe. "I feel like there is a big black cloud hanging over us that doesn't want to move," she said, and I agreed with her. Since February 6, a black cloud of despair had moved in over our town, and with every passing hour the cloud grew darker and heavier.

There was a big crowd in Fleur de Lys. It had been like that from the very beginning. People still came from near and far, bringing Ski-Doos, snowshoes, and anything they might need to take part in the search. Of course, visitors were disappointed to learn that there was little they could do, as everything in town as well as the surrounding countryside had been combed over and over again. Plenty of searching was still being done, for the most part to keep us busy.

Sandwiches, soup, and cooked meals were donated, along with cases of soft drinks. Flowers came in with messages of love and prayers. Every pastor, captain and priest from towns nearby arrived at Sam's home with gifts of food, and with prayers.

A group of men sat at a long table at the hall, speaking with one of the investigators. They wanted to know why the police weren't doing more to have Michael Lewis arrested. Those who had believed all along that he was involved somehow were finally allowing themselves to think that he had in fact killed her. We were frustrated because we felt the police knew more than they were letting on.

The daily routine had been disrupted. No work of any kind was being done. Nobody had any interest in anything aside from going to the hall for updates on Sam, no matter how many times they were greeted with the same news, that there was none. Some were becoming impatient and scared. They wanted something done, and they wanted it done right away. Many wanted to go beyond the law.

Their hands were tied, the officer said, and they had to be careful. "You know," he explained, "the system can seem very difficult to deal with sometimes, especially where teens are concerned. This is going to take time," he added, "and we have to make sure that we do it right."

That same night, February 11, we held a general meeting at the church. The place was overcrowded, and many were left standing outside. The whole town was hungry for new information, anything that might help bring this case to a close. The spokesman for the RCMP opened the meeting by thanking everyone for their cooperation. He went on to report that the dive team had completed their search of the harbour and had found nothing. But, he said, they could be called back on short notice. The chopper had done a lot of searching, but had found no trace of Sam either. Once again we were asked to recall seemingly insignificant details. Anything, he told us, even little things we considered silly. The officers told us that things were going slow, but to be patient.

We needed answers, but there was no one to give them to us. Outside the town hall, a woman said to me that no one in Fleur de Lys was safe. "I feel like there is a big black cloud hanging over us that doesn't want to move," she said, and I agreed with her. Since February 6, a black cloud of despair had moved in over our town, and with every passing hour the cloud grew darker and heavier.

I called George and asked him to come over to my house. That morning I had been talking to a friend, who told me of someone he felt needed to be checked out. I felt that I should discuss this with my brother face to face rather than on the phone. We all assumed our phone lines were being bugged, and I didn't want to disrupt or ruin a person's life by spreading gossip. Whether or not the rumour my friend had told me was true, I still had to talk to George. We could leave no stone unturned; we had to follow every lead, no matter how insignificant it seemed, just like the police officer had said at the meeting.

I hardly knew where to begin. As I looked at George sitting across from me in my armchair, I prayed to God there would be something, anything, I could do for this man. Easing his pain was out of the question. The only thing that could do that was giving him back his baby girl.

I looked away from him.

"George," I said after a pause, "I need to ask you something. I hate to do it, but I have to know."

My brother sat in silence. Finally, he said, "What is it, Gord?"

The words just tumbled out. "Do you think Sam is still alive?"

George answered tearfully, "No, Gord, and I haven't believed that for a while now. I've been lying to myself and hoping that she ran away, but I know this is not so."

It hurt me deeply to hear George say with certainty what I had suspected all along. But from then on, it became a little easier to talk to him about his daughter. That night George admitted he felt Sam was not alive, but he didn't get into who or what he thought might have caused her death. I could only guess how he felt each time Michael Lewis drove by on his ATV.

Shortly after our talk, he had to leave for a meeting in Baie Verte. This was George's and Millie's routine every night since Sam had gone missing. He didn't tell me what the meeting was about or where in Baie Verte it would be held. I assumed it was with the RCMP, for a more detailed briefing on their findings so far.

My mother—Sam's grandmother—moved in with Clo and me soon after Sam disappeared. Mom, who was eighty-one years old, had suffered a stroke two years previous and was unable to do for herself. My sister, Theresa, who had been living with her at the time, moved in with George and Millie, whom we agreed needed her more than Mom did.

Mom could still get around the house without much help, and her mind was sharp. She too felt that by now Sam was dead and that the young man on the ATV was involved. She would sit in her chair by the living room window and stare out at the hills to the west. "I think she is out there somewhere," she would say. "I think there's been an accident."

I didn't want to talk about Sam when my mom was around, but it was difficult when people crowded the house all day and night. Some of the visitors were family and friends, others I knew by first name only, and some were complete strangers. We were happy to have the company, even though all they wanted to talk about was Sam and what might have happened to her.

Mom seemed to sense that I was not happy about all this talk in front of her.

"You don't have to hide anything from me," she said to me one day. "I can take it as well as any one of you."

This made me feel a lot better, and from that moment on we shared every bit of news with her. Many times I saw the tears in her eyes, but I never regretted including her. She was one strong woman.

Kristie told me that one of her friends, a young man, was going to the police station to take a polygraph. It was voluntary on his part, she said, because apparently there was a slight discrepancy in his statement, something to do with the way he answered a question. Now, I thought, here was a young man the police hardly cared about taking a test to clear up some minor detail in his statement to the police. But the person we wanted to take the test wouldn't.

The next time the police came to my house, I was pleased to see it was the same officer who had dropped in twice before. I knew how to treat each policeman by now—who drank coffee or tea, smoked, and so on. The last time he had visited, this officer told me that he'd quit smoking for quite some time, but had recently taken it up again.

Having been a smoker for many years myself, even though I had quit for five years now, I remembered how I used to love to have a cigarette with my coffee. So the first thing I did as he sat at the table was put a mug of coffee, a cigarette and ashtray in front of him. I could tell by the look on his face that this was just what he needed.

The purpose of his visit was not so much to ask questions, but to get to know my own thoughts. He scribbled notes in his writing pad as we talked. First I told him that I felt more strongly that the boy with the ATV was the one involved in Sam's disappearance. I didn't feel at all bad about the second thing I told him. Like many other people—not only in this town, but in a lot of other places—I thought he had murdered her.

"What makes you feel so strongly about this?"

"Well, we all know he was the last person she was seen with," I replied, "and he refuses to take the lie detector test."

He asked me if I thought Michael had something to hide.

"I'm not sure," I told him, "but I think so."

"Have you seen or heard anything new?"

"Yes," I said. "That fellow was never shy about being on the road with his ATV, but you'd think if he saw or heard tell of the police in the area he would be extra careful where he goes on that thing." It was a well-known fact that the main roads were off-limits to all-terrain vehicles. "Now he doesn't seem to care anymore," I continued. "This place is filled with police cars, and that guy is still on the road all the time."

Just then I saw through the window Michael crossing the road on his ATV. He came across to my driveway where the officer's car was parked, turned the trike around, and parked on the road, effectively blocking the cruiser. He just stayed there until the policeman left my house, and as the officer walked from my house down the driveway and around the rear of his car, he found there was very little room to move between the rear of his car and Michael's trike.

I watched in disbelief while the officer started up his vehicle. The boy didn't move to let the car out of the driveway, and the officer had to use extreme caution while backing out, so as not to hit the ATV. Down the street, I could see another police car and a police wagon patrolling the road.

"He is daring the police," I said to Clo.

A lot of people were angry with Michael Lewis and the system that kept him out of reach. We were quickly losing patience, and the police knew it. "Why can't something be done?" one man asked angrily. "Why can't the cops do anything? They feel as well as us the boy is guilty."

"Calm down," another man spoke up. "Like you or I, their hands are tied for the time being. I'm sure if they had enough evidence, this guy would be behind bars."

I informed the two men that I had been talking to one of the officers that morning, who had told me the same thing. Since the boy was a juvenile, they had to be careful; one small mistake could ruin everything. But, I added, there was at least one thing we could do if something didn't break soon. We could do something the police couldn't. The officer had suggested we gather ten or more people and go to this young man's parents and demand their son take the lie detector test.

Clearly, this was not going to be an easy thing to do: to go to any parent and demand what we were sure would be a confession. But time was running out. For all we knew, Sam could be out there hurt or starving, and Michael was the key to us finding her. Then an even more horrible thought intruded on my thoughts. What if some other boy or girl went missing while we were looking for Sam?

Suddenly I wasn't afraid anymore. I would do what had to be done if and when the time came.

I had a hard time going to Samantha's house. It broke my heart to be around her parents. It had gotten a little easier to talk to George since the day he admitted he feared his daughter was dead, but so sad to see Millie. I could barely look at the woman, she was so distraught. I'd never in my life seen two people with so much hurt and pain on their faces. I tried to keep my visits short, as I felt so helpless in their presence.

George gave me an e-mail to read. It had come from a friend who knew a psychic living in the United States. The story of the missing girl from Fleur de Lys was being heard all over North America now, and letters and calls from abroad came as a comfort.

In the letter, the psychic described a young boy with an ATV, giving as good a description of Michael Lewis as if she'd lived in Fleur de Lys all her life. She said not to bother with the bus shelter, because he did not put her off there. Sam was hours from Fleur de Lys, the letter went on to say, near running water and an old shack. The chopper had flown over her but missed her due to malfunctions.

I could sense Michael's father was getting more and more nervous as time passed. He spent a lot of time helping out with the search, but he was acting strangely. He would stare out the window for a long time, looking as if he were in a world of his own. It seemed he couldn't settle in any one place for long. Often, he would come into the hall and not sit or speak, but just turn around and leave in a hurry.

I pitied him, and I wasn't the only one. I tried to imagine what it was like to be in his situation. How would I feel if my son had last been seen with Sam, and with the police dogging him for answers? All we had to go on was Michael's word.

His father must have had some idea what was on everyone's mind. His son was in trouble, and he knew it. But one question nagged me about the father. Did he also know what was on his son's mind?

I didn't see his mother as often. She worked full-time at a store and I only caught the occasional glimpse of her. I used to see her take early-morning walks with Millie, sometimes as early as 5:30 A.M. She seemed to be a quiet and shy person. She had babysat Sam quite a bit while Millie worked as a schoolteacher and George a fish plant operator.

I believe this woman loved Sam just as she loved her own children. And by this time she must have known what the police and the residents suspected her son had done. I could only guess what this poor lady must have been feeling.

Chapter 5

At night, when I finally went to bed, I would lie wide awake thinking about Sam, when suddenly Michael would pop into my mind. Try as I might, I could not rid him from my thoughts. I could imagine him doing things to her, and I was helpless to rid myself of these thoughts. I could picture her, a frightened little child, trying to break away, crying and calling for her dad, knowing in her young mind that this was insane, and that she was going to die...

Sam had been gone over a week now, and still there were no leads. By the way the police were talking, they believed foul play was involved. Most residents of Fleur de Lys had been feeling this way for the past few days and they also believed that Michael was responsible.

But the teenagers who went to school with him wouldn't believe this. I spoke to some kids who hung around with him. I asked them if their friend was capable of hurting Sam.

No, came the answer.

Michael's schoolmates said they knew he was bad and that he was not scared of much, but to be responsible for Sam's disappearance? To lead the whole town and the police on a wild goose chase? This they didn't believe.

They asked if I had seen him lately, and I would tell them that, yes, I see him every day. "Well," they asked me, "does he look like a person who has done something like that?"

"No, he doesn't," I lied.

The children of Fleur de Lys were going through a much harder time than anyone realized. First of all, one of their friends was gone and might never be seen alive again. As if that weren't enough, another of their friends was being watched by the police as a suspect in her disappearance. Perhaps they were hurting most of all.

Soon the police returned to my house for more questions. I was happy to see the officer I had spoken to before. Right away I noticed he was getting more frustrated by the tone of his voice and the way he carried himself. He repeated the same questions as before, and afterwards he talked more openly and sounded sure this time that Michael Lewis was guilty of murder.

"The last time you were here," I reminded him, "you thought it might be an accident."

Now, he said, the entire police force believed they had a murderer on their hands. I asked if they had anything concrete to back this up. He ignored the question and asked for another cup of coffee. His patience was clearly cracking. Every time the young man's name was mentioned, his expression changed. Once, when I spoke Michael Lewis's name, he winced and said, "He is going to be grabbed soon, and I promise Jesus, when he is, he will talk."

But it was all talk and he knew it. They needed the young man to confess, but they couldn't force him to do it. I didn't know it at the time, but this would be the last time the police officer visited my house. I always looked forward to his company. He was a decent fellow, and I enjoyed talking with him.

Across the road from my house, at the town hall which we were now calling headquarters, the feeling was that we would soon get a break. When I asked people what they had heard, they replied they had heard nothing new. But somehow anticipation was in the air.

There was a police officer in the hall who seemed to be busy, but I asked him if I could have a word. He was new to me; I hadn't seen him before. I asked him why everyone seemed so sure there was going to be a break in the investigation. Had the police found anything new he could tell me?

"Mr. Walsh," he said, "I'm sorry for the trouble you and your family are having. It must be a terrible thing, especially in a small town."

I agreed. I told him that it was about to get worse, too. If all our suspicions were correct, Sam was not only missing but dead, and the murderer was walking around town as if he were on a holiday.

"To answer your question," he said, not commenting at all on what we thought, "we haven't seen or heard anything that would make the people think there's a break in the case. In cases such as this, people want a break so badly they get together and create their own outcomes. After a while, they believe what they want to believe." He assured me that everything that could be done was being done, and that in the end there would be a break. It just might not come as quickly as they would like.

Of course he was right. What could be done was very little, but I had faith in the police and their abilities. Forcing Michael to confess was out of the question, and he knew it as well as we did. The only thing the authorities could do at this point was to keep the pressure on him. But for all that, he seemed to be having the time of his life nowadays, enjoying himself more than ever.

Most felt Samantha was dead, some expressing the thought openly that she would never be seen again. Some believed that she had been taken somewhere along the coastline and dumped in the ocean. If so, there was a good chance she was never going to be found.

I hoped this wasn't the case. If her body was found, of course we would feel sad, but at least there would be some kind of closure to this terrible affair. George and Millie in time might live some kind of normal life without their loving daughter. But if she were never found, then there would be no end to the fear the people in Fleur de Lys felt. We would never know if there was a murderer in our midst, and there would be no peace for George, Millie, and Sam's brother Sandy.

While talking to some visitors at my home one day, someone I didn't know looked out the window and said, "There he goes on that goddamned trike again."

"I'd like to see someone burn that goddamned thing," he continued, "because it makes me sick to my stomach to look at it. I don't see why the police haven't taken that trike before this." Then, as if correcting himself, he said, "I guess they've got a reason for not doing it."

"Yes," I said, "I think they know what they're doing."

One of my friends then recounted a conversation he had had with a police officer. The officer had told him there wasn't much they could do with the young man without his cooperation and the consent from the parents. He said they kept putting pressure on his parents to try and convince their son to take the lie detector test, but that was about all they could do.

There seemed to be no end to people's goodness. Along with the food came prayers and cards from every church and organization in the province. People travelled from great distances just to talk to George and Millie and try to comfort them. Many who came to town knew them, and many didn't. Some felt they shouldn't talk to George and Millie, so they came by my place to to give me messages for my brother and his wife. The search parties kept growing daily as new volunteers arrived.

Early one morning, a stranger arrived unannounced at my brother's house. He introduced himself and said he was from Pilley's Island. He had driven all the way down to speak with George and Millie. He told them that they had been on his mind since Sam went missing, and that last night he hadn't slept at all, so...here he was. He had a few words with those present, said a prayer, then left for his long drive home. I was touched by his show of kindness.

People phoned not only from Newfoundland and the rest of Canada, but from all over the world. A lot of those calls were from people who didn't know us or hadn't even heard of Fleur de Lys until Samantha's story got on the airwaves. Many calls came to my home, some by mistake, others because the callers couldn't get through to George's, and some because they felt awkward phoning Sam's parents out of the blue. But whether they got my home or George's, they all called for the same reason. Every one said the same thing, that if George and Millie needed anything, they should not hesitate to call.

The investigators seemed to be showing an awful lot of interest in the bus shelter once again. There were about half a dozen police officers with some local men on the road in front of the little structure, removing snow and ice. After melting the snow and ice with a tiger torch, they studied the ground very carefully.

I spoke to the officer in charge. He told me they were looking for anything they could find, not any one particular thing. "We need something to work with besides that young man," he said, "and the only thing we can do without him is search."

"It's a well-known fact that the investigation has come to a stop," I said in an accusing tone, "that everyone is still on the move, but more for show than anything else."

We talked for some time while they finished melting the ice and looking everything over. I watched angrily as they swept the area with a metal detector. Twice they got a sound, but both times it turned out to be just tiny nails. This operation was a bust as well, owing partly to the bad weather. The late afternoon had brought nothing but newly fallen wet snow and bitter disappointment.

At night, when I finally went to bed, I would lie wide awake thinking about Sam, when suddenly Michael would pop into my mind. Try as I might, I could not rid him from my thoughts. I could imagine him doing things to her, and I was helpless to rid myself of these thoughts. I could picture her, a frightened little child, trying to break away, crying and calling for her dad, knowing in her young mind that this was insane, and that she was going to die...

And then I would suddenly think, *My God! What if I am wrong about him?*

For I had nothing concrete to go on, only that he was the last one seen with her. If I am wrong, I thought, how would I be able to look him in the eye again after accusing him of murdering Sam? I had already accused him in front of many people. I prayed that if I was wrong about him God would forgive me.

Chapter 6

I was making coffee for everyone when the phone rang. I picked up the receiver. A friend of mine was on the other end, asking me if I had heard the news. I told him I had watched the seven o'clock news.

"No, no," he said. "They've found Sam."

The weather this morning reminded me of the first week Sam had gone missing. A heavy snowfall had covered the ground then, too. Like every other morning, the sound of Ski-Doos revving up pierced the air. Michael Lewis would be smiling today. There were no more trails to follow and no tracks to be seen, due to the thick blanket of snow on the ground. Any clues or signs that we had so far overlooked were now hopelessly lost.

Rumours still floated around town, most of them old, all of them checked and rechecked, and finally ruled out by the investigators. I talked to one person who believed Sam had gone to the boat in the harbour and either jumped or fallen in. He believed this because there were sneaker tracks on its rail. Someone had the idea that the people from the boat had taken her, not in the boat, but in the red car that had been brought here specifically for that purpose. The theory was pursued, and the owners of the boat questioned. But there was nothing more to it than some fisherman wanting to leave his boat tied up at the wharf.

Soon after Sam's disappearance, I had overheard someone say that Sam was a smart kid, that she had planned the whole thing and that her parents would receive a ransom note in two to three days. I never believed a word of it, and I couldn't believe some people would be so callous to suggest such a thing.

Sam's grandmother would still gaze toward the northwest hills of Fleur de Lys. "Poor Sam is in there somewhere," she would say just as she had done so many time before. "I think it was an accident."

From early morning 'til late at night, people filled my home. For the past two weeks we had sat together, trying to pass the time, talking about the only thing that interested us these days. The questions were not so much where Sam was or what had happened to her. They were more often "What did he do to her?" or "Where has he hidden her?"

We all felt lost and alone.

I was making coffee for everyone when the phone rang. I picked up the receiver. A friend of mine was on the other end, asking me if I had heard the news. I told him I had watched the seven o'clock news.

"No, no," he said. "They've found Sam."

My heart stopped.

"Gord, are you okay?"

"Yes," I replied. "Where did they find her?"

He didn't know any more than that Samantha Walsh had been found, but he would let me know when he learned more.

When I laid the receiver down, I noticed the room had become deathly quiet. Everyone knew that something important had just happened, and they all looked at me with expectant faces.

"The call was about Sam," I said. "They found her."

Questions were thrown at me in rapid-fire. Who found her? Where is she? Their words sounded vague and distant to me. I had no answers.

Soon the telephone was ringing constantly. People called wanting to know if it was true: Had we found Sam? I had to tell them that I was sorry but I could tell them nothing. I didn't know any more than they did. In less than two hours, we received calls from British Columbia, Ontario and St. John's.

Someone phoned us from Port Hardy, BC, and told us she had heard a report that Samantha Walsh's body had been found in an old mine shaft. Then a friend of mine called to report that Sam had been found in the cemetery. I told my friend about the call from Port Hardy and asked him for the source of his information. Later that night, we received a different story. This one said she had been found out of town, next to the side of the high road.

Finding Sam's body was what everyone expected, but not what anyone wanted. One of our dear children was dead, and there was nothing we could do to bring her back. That night, one of Sam's cousins received the news from a store clerk. It was a shame he had to hear the news this way, that the little girl from Fleur de Lys had been found.

It looked like Michael Lewis's days were numbered now. The body had been found, and now the law would be able to confirm that a crime had been committed. We knew in our hearts all along that she was dead, that she had been murdered, and furthermore who had done the deed. We weren't worried that the autopsy would prove us wrong—the only thing on our minds was what would become of young Michael Lewis.

With more calls coming in and more conflicting stories of where Sam had been found, I began to feel that something was wrong. I needed to get to the bottom of it. If the reports turned out to be false, our hopes of bringing Michael to justice would be dashed. It's not easy meeting a fellow on the road three or four times a day, to look through your window and see him running about and doing as he pleases, while suspecting that this person has killed a child.

I knew where I had to go to get the truth, but I couldn't bring myself to go down to George's. My brother had already been sure his daughter was dead, but today's news would break his heart.

Going out of my mind with worry, I finally found the nerve to call George's house. As luck would have it, someone answered. I asked the woman on the line if it was true, if they had found Sam. My heart was in my throat as she spoke to me in a very calm voice. She didn't know how these rumours got started, but that's all it was, a rumour. Sam had not been found.

The lady told me there were calls coming from all over Newfoundland and the rest of Canada and that the phones were ringing off the hook. I told her the same thing was happening here. "But before you hang up," I said, "I want to know how George and Millie are doing."

"They aren't saying very much," she replied, "but you can tell they're very upset."

The next day I spoke to one of the police officers and asked him where the rumour had come from. Some people were saying the police themselves were behind it. He told me that he didn't have any idea where it came from.

"Too bad it's not true," he remarked. "It would have made it easier for us to get the killer off the street."

"It looks like we're back to square one," I said disgustedly.

I could feel the anger and frustration in the air when I entered the town hall. The place was packed with residents of Fleur de Lys screaming for answers. "What's the good of the goddamned law," one man said to me, "if they can't take that young fucker and make him talk? They should at least get him off the street and lock him up." Before I could answer, he continued, "I know their hands are tied and they're doing everything they can do legally, but I am so pissed off. I have a young one about Sam's age, and I'm scared."

I told him that I knew how he felt. "I have a daughter, too," I said. "She's older, but I still have the worry, the same as you do."

"What will we do if no body is ever found?" he asked.

I had to admit I didn't know what we could do. I told him there were lots of cases like this, where the body was never found, or not until many years had passed.

"Yes, you're right about that," he said. "But in most of those cases they don't know if the person is dead or alive. It's not like that here. I know that girl is dead and

I know who is involved in it, and the worst part about it is that he's sitting and eating at this table with us right here in this hall."

"I see it that way, too," I told him. "If Sam's body isn't found, we may have to live like this for a long time."

Just then another man pulled up on his Ski-Doo and came through the open door. I hadn't seen him for three or four days, and he, like everyone else in the town and all over the country, wanted to know what was happening. I asked him what he thought of the stories that had been spread all over Canada.

"I never in my life knew of anything that got so much attention as this," he spat. "I think it would have been great to get that scum off the street. We all know who it is, but we can't do a fuckin' thing about it."

I asked him how things were for him in general.

"Not good," he said. "We can't sleep, myself and my wife. We spend most nights walking the floor or just sitting looking at each other. I'm drinking more whisky than I should, and I've picked up smoking again. I've cried more times in the last two weeks than I've cried in my entire lifetime, and I'm not eating properly. I find I can't work; all I can do is think. I was supposed to start cutting my firewood this morning, but when I got to my cutting area, I stopped and just sat on my Ski-Doo, smoked two cigarettes and looked at the trees and thought about Millie and George and poor young Sam.

"I realized there wasn't a sound to be heard except the west wind. Normally, this time of day and this time of year there would be chainsaws roaring all around me, and Ski-Doos going in and out of the woods. But this time there was nothing, not a sound. That's when the sickening thought hit me; we have a killer among us. Then I pulled the cord, and here I am."

He stared off into space and said, "I wonder if that young man even cares a tiny little bit about what he has done?"

There came talk of a reward. There wouldn't be any problem raising money, but some of us thought that it wasn't such a great idea. When money is offered, it interests people who don't care about missing children or broken-hearted moms and dads. I, for one, did not agree with a reward being posted. Once the word was out, we would be receiving distracting calls from all parts of Newfoundland and across Canada, maybe even from other parts of the world. For now it was only talk, and I hoped it was going to be just that for a little longer.

However, a good number of people in Fleur de Lys wanted the reward posted as quickly as possible. They still felt that someone had seen or heard something, and that money might bring them forward. I didn't believe that at all. I told them I didn't think there was anyone with Michael when he had taken Sam and that I felt everyone had told the police all they could—all except this one young man, and no amount of money was going to make him talk. I further argued that, even if he did have help, it was unlikely a reward would make his accomplice talk. The truth would get leaked anyway, hopefully sometime in the near future.

"It's not in the future we want answers," one supporter of the reward money idea said. "It's right now." When people get scared enough, they want to forge ahead with any plan that offers a quick solution. We were torn. On the one hand, offering a reward might bring someone forward right away. But I thought this scheme would almost certainly get in the way of the investigation.

Michael Lewis's family were going through a very hard time. One of his sisters was my daughter's best friend, and had been since they were old enough to walk. She had spent countless hours at my home, listening to music and hanging out in Kristie's room. She was the kind of girl anyone would like their daughter to be friends with. But since Sam went missing, Kristie's friend had only come around a couple of times.

On her last visit she had stayed for two hours, but she didn't look like the same girl at all. She seemed frightened, like there was something on her mind. She talked about Sam's disappearance, how she had been like a sister to her, how her mom used to babysit Sam and that she had stayed overnight at the Walsh's house. No one interrupted her while she spoke; we knew she was having a very hard time. They were asking her brother a lot of questions, she said. I could detect a quiver in her voice and a slight tremor in her hands.

I did not see her and Michael's mother very often—maybe on the road taking her walk or going to the grocery store—but I saw more of their dad than ever before. He still looked very nervous, never staying in one place for more than a minute or two. Every time I saw him, there were tears in his eyes. He wasn't talking very much, though he often went to the town hall with everyone else. But of course he wouldn't stay very long.

I tried to put myself in his shoes, tried to think what he might be thinking. But I couldn't. His son was public enemy number one. And I suspected even he knew more than he was saying.

I'd say he was scared of what was coming.

TOP: Saltwater girl Samantha Walsh.
BOTTOM LEFT: Samantha the angel.
BOTTOM RIGHT: Samantha Walsh and her brother Sandy, with their parents George and Millie Walsh.

Samantha Walsh in a familiar pose, looking out over the water.

TOP: The bus shelter where Michael Lewis told the police he left Samantha Walsh on the night she went missing.
BOTTOM: Police divers searching the frozen waters of Fleur de Lys.

TOP: (L-R) RCMP Officers Paddy McNeil, Corporal B. Division, Serious Crime Unit West, and Sergeant Bruce Williams, Operations Commander, Team Leader (Baie Verte) BOTTOM: (L-R) Frank Rumbolt, Winston Anstey of the Deer Lake volunteer Search and Rescue team.

TOP: Tracker Leonardo Caldi and his bloodhound Gypsy.
BOTTOM: Gypsy led searchers to this cabin. Hours later, Samantha Walsh's body was found approximately thirty feet away.

TOP: Samantha Walsh's body being placed in hearse as her parents look on.
BOTTOM LEFT: Bill Barrett comforts his daughter during Samantha's funeral.
BOTTOM RIGHT: Today, young and old alike visit Samantha's grave.

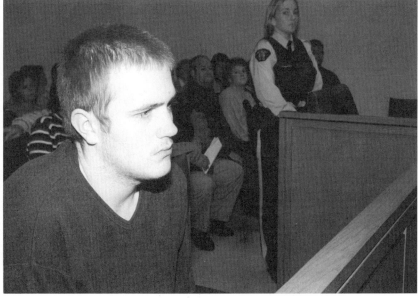

TOP: First court appearance of Michael Lewis.
BOTTOM: Michael John Victor Lewis was found guilty of second-degree murder.
(Courtesy of *The Western Star*)

Eulogy by Father Edward Brophy
at the funeral of Samantha Bertha Walsh 1986-2000,
held in St. Theresa's Roman Catholic Church
in Fleur de Lys, Newfoundland

"Fleur de Lys.

"A Flower.

"A Lily.

"Consider the lilies of the field. Will the flowers ever grow in Fleur de Lys again? Think about the flowers. Consider the lilies of the field." But will the flowers ever grow here again? Will the earth refuse to give her beauty—her fragrance?

"During World War II, in one of the German concentration camps, 15,000 children were brought to one camp but only 100 left it alive. A young girl, a young teenaged girl wrote these lines:

"The world's abloom, and seems to smile.

"I want to fly, but where, how high?

"If in barbed wire things can bloom

"Why couldn't I? I will not die."

"To a young woman—or a child—all things may seem possible. But will the flowers ever grow in Fleur de Lys again?

"Think about the flowers. A life may be like a flower. Every life, and every flower is unique, different, special.

"Every flower, every life, mirrors the beauty of the creator.

"And some flowers, and some lives, bloom quickly and are gone.

"But each flower is most radiant before it dies.

"Think about the flowers.

"We could be overwhelmed by the sadness of all this—overcome by the ugliness of it all. But we may recall the Easter Lily—tall, elegant, fragrant, white—a flower, a lily like a trumpet—shouting that Jesus is risen. The Easter Lily is the symbol of the risen Christ. Yet—this gorgeous flower begins with an ugly—a rough brown bulb.

"We are a people of hope. We are a people of faith. We believe in Jesus, who is the Resurrection and the Life. So we look beyond this present sad time—this ugly moment—to a new life in the Risen Jesus.

"We are gathered in this humble Newfoundland church, a church dedicated to St. Theresa, the Little Flower, whom we love so much. And St. Theresa promised: 'I will let fall from heaven a shower of roses.' And this will happen!

"Last Friday I buried an old man in Harbour Round. After Mass I went to the graveyard and blessed the grave. I came back into the church and as I walked up the aisle, there on the carpet, a beautiful red rose. And I did not say: 'It fell off the coffin.' I didn't say: 'It fell from a bouquet.' But immediately, I thought, as I picked it up: 'St. Theresa. She has started already. I will let fall from heaven a shower of roses.'

"So do not weep or mourn for this little girl. For we believe that she is another fair flower in God's beautiful bouquet. Rather: This I ask: Plant flowers. Plant seeds: pansies, roses, forget-me-nots, lilies. And of the young I ask: Plant seeds, good seeds, seeds of Holiness and Healing, seeds of compassion and forgiveness, with their roots deep in Christ. And I ask this: uproot all the seeds and weeds of ugliness and bitterness and anger. This little girl would not want a legacy of bitterness or a trail of ugliness.

"If we are not an example to the world now: Jesus died in vain. And so did Samantha.

"Dear children, plant seeds, plant flowers. The earth will forgive. Plant good seeds, and when people come here in the summer, they will cry: "Oh! The beautiful flowers of Fleur de Lys.""

Dear Walsh Family,

I am a fourteen-year-old girl from Norman's Cove. I did not know Samantha or her family but I feel the need to write this, praying that it would be encouragement to you.

My heart goes out to you and the community of Fleur de Lys through such a great loss. I've been following the news recently and have seen you, the parents, expressing your thoughts, and it breaks my heart to know that you just lost your thirteen-year-old daughter.

Through the news, I've seen videos of Samantha as a kid, have heard her sing, and have seen how much of an impact she made on her school and whole community. When I say my prayers at night, I remember asking God why such a thing has happened to such a young, wonderful girl. But God has helped me to understand that we may not always have an answer for all that happens as it happens right away, but in time, he'll help us to understand and forgive. God's son Jesus was killed and he did nothing wrong. He only did good, his mother also must have asked, Why? Why? She didn't understand then, but she understood afterwards. We may not know why this happened to Samantha, but one day we will understand it all.

Most of all, I think about how fortunate she now is. She's living in heaven, under God's precious arms, wrapped around her, safe and sound, instead of in this world, on this earth, that is full of sin. She is so blessed. Sammy may not be with you in person today, but I know she lives in her heart and she always will. But because I didn't know her, I picture her as an angel, and she's in heaven. She's looking down on her parents and asking that they would not cry, for now she is so happy, she's with God, and when God calls her parents, she wants them to be ready too.

I hope, in some way, that this letter has brought some peace to your life. I pray that it has given you strength to continue on to tomorrow. The prayers and thoughts of my family, myself, and my church are with you all.

My prayer tonight is that you would find peace in knowing that your daughter is in heaven, looking down upon you.

Love & Prayers
Susan Newhook
& Family

Feb. 29

I went to visit Sam at the funeral home tonight. It's been 23 days since she has gone missing. I touched her silky hair, looked at her pretty face, and I asked God why.

She is so young to lose her life. If it had been an accident or sickness I could accept it, but for one of our friends to take her life, it's like a horror story.

Sam came home to Fleur de Lys tonight. It has taken her so long to get home since she left Nan's on Feb. 6. It isn't a happy homecoming for us

March 2

I woke up this morning and, as usual, Sam was the first thing on my mind, she never leaves it. I'm sure she never leaves the mind of anyone in Fleur de Lys. I looked out the window at the big birch tree by our house, its branches were all bent with ice. They looked so beautiful, to me it seemed to say God was sharing our sorrow by bending the trees and branches to show us, our whole community, He knows what we are going through.

It will never be the same again here in our safe haven, where we thought there was no evil, no cruelty, no one would harm us. I pray to God that with time we will heal. Please God with time and all the prayers Uncle George, Aunt Millie and Sandy will heal also.

Tomorrow on March 3, we will say a final goodbye to Sam, but she will live forever in our hearts.

Cousin Kristie (17 years old)

Saltwater Joys
(Samantha's Song)

Just to wake up in the morning
To the quiet of the cove
And hear Aunt Bessie talkin' to herself
And hear poor Uncle John
Mumbling wishes to Old Nell
It made me feel like everything was fine

Refrain:

I was born down by the water
It's here I'm gonna stay
I've searched for all the reasons
Why I should go away
But I haven't got the thirst
For all those modern day toys
So I'll just take my chances
With those saltwater joys

Following a little brook as it trickles to the shore
In the autumn when the trees are flaming red
Kicking leaves that fall around me
Watching sunset paint the hills
It's all I'll ever need to feel at home

This island that we cling to
Has been handed down with pride
By folks that fought to live here
Taking hardships all in stride
So I'll compliment her beauty
Hold on to my goodbyes
And I'll stay and take my chances with those
Saltwater joys

How can I leave those mornings
With the sunrise on the cover
And the gulls like flies
Surrounding Clayton's wharf
Flatter's Island wrapped in rainbows
In the evening after fog
The ocean's smells are perfume to my soul

So I'm going to where the buildings
Reach beneath the clouds
Where warm and gentle people
Turn to swarm and faceless people
So I'll do without the riches
Glamour and the noise
And I'll stay and take my chances
With those saltwater joys

Written by Wayne Chaulk and performed by Buddy Wasisname and the Other Fellers. Used with permission from Third Wave Productions.

Chapter 7

"My God, Gord," she blurted out, "I've talked to almost every person in this town, and they all think like you do. But me, I can't believe that the young man we're talking about would do such a thing as take someone and kill them, and then hide them! Isn't that what you are saying?"

"Yes," I said, "that's exactly what I am saying."

Every night since February 6, George, Millie, Millie's brother Jim Lewis, and Paul Shelley, the Member of the House of Assembly for Baie Verte–White Bay, would meet with the police at their Baie Verte office for a briefing on the day's findings. George and Millie would only tell us what the police allowed them to say. One thing they didn't have to tell us was that the investigation was not going well.

We could see for ourselves that the police were running out of places to look. Everything had been checked over and over again. Every place had been searched from top to bottom. The officers still continued interviewing every individual in town over and over, hoping against hope that someone might remember something they had forgotten to include in their earlier statements.

People started to raise money for a reward. Roy Barker, businessman from Baie Verte, had volunteered to take the responsibility of receiving calls and keeping records of all the pledges. Some of the larger businesses were pledging anywhere from five to ten thousand dollars. Smaller firms pledged as high as a thousand. The reward figure climbed high into the tens of thousands, but I was relieved to hear that the police wanted the announcement of a reward put off until a later date.

"We all know what money can do," one officer told me. "There will be a lot of time wasted taking calls with tips that lead nowhere." He allowed that it might be helpful sometime in the future. In the meantime, Mr. Barker was determined to raise as much money as possible. He was getting the information out any way possible, I heard him say over a radio news show.

For the past two weeks, I had made many trips to the town hall for news. Each time, I moved through the crowd to where the people in charge were sitting. And each time, I asked the same question: What's the news today? The sad, tired, sick look, the shake of the head, and the words "not a word" were becoming all too familiar to me these days. Today as I entered the hall, everyone was talking about the reward that was going to be posted. "It's the best grease to loosen the town," one woman observed. Others were not so sure.

I glanced around the room. At a table against the wall, eating a sandwich and drinking from a styrofoam cup, sat Michael Lewis. I watched him with mounting anger, knowing that he held all the answers. I said as much to the man sitting next to me, one of those who disagreed with the reward. He patted my shoulder. "You can bet your bottom dollar he's not going to tell us anything," he said.

The young man finished his lunch, stood up and made a show of stretching, as if he wanted to be noticed. He moved through the crowd, listening and saying very little to the comments made about him. Some men and women said that a person had to be awfully cold-hearted to do such a thing to Sam and hide it for so long. Others referred to the perpetrator as a "scumbag," saying what they'd like to do to him. Michael would have had to be deaf not to hear this. But he wasn't, and I hoped it was making him mad.

He was doing a good job covering up. After a few minutes, he walked out the door as if he hadn't a care in the world. His dad was sitting at one of the other tables with his head bent, picking at some small object in his hand. He seemed to be in a world of his own. To sit like he was for five minutes was a long time for him since this all began. He stood, said his goodbyes, then followed his son outdoors.

There were close to a hundred people sitting inside and standing outside the entrance, men and women and lots of children. Everyone was muttering angrily about Michael and what they'd like to do to him. One man cleared his throat and the talking stopped.

"I have reached the end of my rope," the man announced, "and from what I'm getting from the rest of you, you feel the same way."

There was a murmur of consent.

"I feel the same as you do," said a man who was a stranger to me, "but what can we do?"

"I know what might get him to talk," the first man said, "but if I were to do what I'm thinking, those two guys would have the cuffs on me right now." He pointed to two police officers sitting at a table writing, or perhaps listening and just pretending to be busy.

"Maybe we should ask the police for some advice," I offered.

With that, the two police officers looked up from their papers. They exchanged a look before one of them spoke. "At this point in time we have done everything we can," he said. "It's very clear who you think is responsible for what's happened to the young girl. We think, like you do, that the young man in question was involved in Sam's disappearance, but we have to be very careful what we do and say. If he's the one, then he is a young offender and this ties our hands. If it turns out he's the one and we make a mistake, then all our work—yours and ours—would have been for nothing. We've worked our asses off for months on other cases and arrested the ones we were a hundred per cent sure were guilty, brought them into court, and because of some silly human mistake they were set free. Believe me, we don't want that."

His partner spoke up. "What you people can do is very limited as well," he explained, "but you could try and pressure his parents to have him take the polygraph."

The clock on the wall read 5:45. There was a TV at the hall, but I wanted to be home for the six o'clock news, where I could watch in peace. That evening my mother watched the news beside me. She, as well as the rest of us, was anxiously waiting to hear of any new developments in the case. For two weeks now, the Samantha Walsh story was the top news item in all the local media.

The clock on the wall struck six, and the evening news was on. Sam's now-famous picture appeared on the screen at the very beginning, and the journalist said that nothing new had happened in the search for the girl from Fleur de Lys. They flashed some pictures of the town: the area where Sam was last seen on the ice, her grandmother's house, the icy spots under which the divers had searched.

Every day the reporters went around Fleur de Lys busily putting stories together. And always their task was the same—to report that there was nothing new. Each day they stopped people on the roads or in grocery stores. Some people wouldn't talk on camera; often I saw people shaking their heads and walking away. Tonight, the news was just another in a long line of disappointments.

Whenever Sam's picture came on the TV screen, I glanced at my mother and saw the hurt and misery come into her eyes. "Poor Sam," she would say, "I wonder where she is?"

I usually said nothing. There weren't any words that could take away her pain. Only one thing could do that for her, and that was for her granddaughter to walk in.

My mother's eighty-first birthday, February 10, had come four days after Sam and George and Millie had sat down to supper with Mom and the rest of us, four days after Sam had left first because she had some homework to do for the next day, four days after the last day she was seen alive. As a family, we tried to help her celebrate, but our hearts weren't in it, and neither was hers. That was the day when people started getting brave enough to start rumours, that Sam had run away or was kidnapped. That day had seen George interviewed on television, begging his daughter to come home or at least call her nan to wish her a happy birthday.

After the news, I asked Mom what she thought had happened to Sam. I don't know what possessed me to ask her, because I knew what she was going to say. She had said the same thing before.

"I'm afraid someone's got Sam," she said, wiping her eyes, "and I'm afraid they are hurting her."

On day fifteen, Monday morning, I crossed the road to the town hall. I could tell there was nothing new even before I asked the question. But I would ask the question anyway, and people there would just hunch their shoulders and shake their heads, with a sad, worn-out look on their faces. They too had lived through fifteen days with very little sleep.

There was one interesting development, though. For the last couple of days, a chopper had been surveying the area beyond the bus shelter, towards the hills north of town. This is the direction the boy copying on the ice with his friends had seen Sam being taken on the trike. He had said many times that the ATV didn't stop at the bus shelter, but that it followed on over the hills. I learned that Michael Lewis had become very interested in the evening news while the chopper searched the hills.

Day fifteen dragged on like all the rest, cold and dreary, for that black cloud that hung over our once happy town was getting darker all the time. That night at the hall, I sat with a dozen or so people sitting at a long table, each one there going over events and trying to make some sense out of them.

"Like it or not," I said, "we're going to have to do what the police had suggested." They knew what I meant. We would have to confront Michael's parents and insist they force their son to take the lie detector test. In fact, I couldn't believe it had taken us this long to do it.

"I was in favour of doing this four or five days ago," one of the men told me. "How much longer are we going to wait? You know as well as I do we have a murdering beast among us. We don't know when he'll strike again."

We decided to form a group of men and women the next day and do what had to be done. Before our little informal meeting was adjourned, I told them we would need a spokesman to do the talking. We didn't want to go to this man's house and have ten or twelve people all speaking at once. It had to be done in a quiet and sensible manner.

On my way home late that night, I met a man as he was leaving my house. He must have had a special reason for calling, because he wasn't one to come to my house at this hour. In fact, he hardly came to my house at all.

"Your wife said I would find you at the hall," he said.

I asked him what was up.

"I don't know if there's anything to it or not," he said. "It may just be another rumour."

I assured him a rumour was probably better than anything I had heard all day.

"I overheard someone say Michael Lewis is going to Baie Verte tomorrow to take the lie detector test."

I became excited. He must have noticed this, even in the dark. "Hey, take it easy," he said. "There may be nothing to it."

"No, man, this has got to be real," I said. "This will be our first real break."

I hadn't been getting much sleep since the sixth, and that night I had none at all. I prayed like I'd never prayed before, that Michael would take the polygraph and answer all our questions. I'd been thinking about going to his father's house for many days, and the more I thought about it, the more I hated the idea. He lived very close to where I lived, and no matter what happened, we would still have to live as neighbours after this was all over.

In the beginning, the town hall was kept open twenty-four hours, but for the past few nights they were closing the place somewhere between ten and midnight, and opening it again at seven the next morning. The police urged people to go home and get some sleep, arguing that there wasn't much they could do after midnight anyway.

The investigators would routinely leave Fleur de Lys each evening at ten and drive to Baie Verte, returning each morning at eight-thirty. Some of the more desperate townspeople felt the authorities should be on the job much earlier in the morning and much later at night. One fellow who was thinking more clearly than the rest was quick to defend the officers. "I don't think it's fair to come down on those guys like that," he said. "They're doing the best they can. Besides, they need their sleep the same as we do—in fact, they need it more. They have to be very alert and have to keep their minds sharp." And that was the last time I heard the police being criticized.

Morning was slow coming. I was eager for someone to open the door to the town hall. People came to the hall in ever greater numbers. Today there were more police cars and police trucks than ever before. One huge truck with SEARCH AND RESCUE written on the side in large letters sat near the hall. I asked the driver what it was doing here. He told me they got the order last night to be in Fleur de Lys in the morning. "We have some high-tech equipment on board," he said. "Any more than that, I can't tell you."

I soon learned they were going into the country to do some investigating at an old cabin that I never know existed. A man from town had built the place two or three years earlier and abandoned it when he moved away. Some of the local teenagers had taken over the place, and during winter this was where they hung out and partied. Michael Lewis had spent a great deal of time there, I heard.

The police didn't tell anyone what, if anything, they found at the cabin. They might have found something, perhaps some fingerprints, that led them to believe Sam had been there, but they remained tight-lipped. They began asking whether Sam had been to the cabin at any time prior to her disappearance. George called me and asked if I would question my daughter Kristie to find out if Sam had ever gone to the cabin. This was the only hint that they might have found something.

So far I had been unable to confirm anything about Michael taking the lie detector test, so I made my way toward some officious-looking people in the town hall. There were two strangers at this table with Tom Walsh, our fire chief. I guessed they were policemen. For the past few days, I had seen a lot of strangers moving around town whom I assumed were investigators.

"What's new?" I asked Tom just as I did every morning. He just shook his head as usual, but I noticed a different expression on his face today. I didn't ask him what I really wanted to ask. Instead, I left and made my way to see if a certain truck had left town yet.

After an hour that seemed like forever, the vehicle finally passed my place, heading in the direction of Baie Verte. It may not have meant much; they could be heading anywhere. But then I caught a glimpse of Michael Lewis sitting inside, and my hopes got ever higher.

"God", I said, "He's going to take the test."

By 1:30 P.M., every person in town was talking in excited tones about Michael and the polygraph. They were not coming right out and saying it, but, like me, they all thought it might be a breakthrough. A crowd of people sat around my kitchen table with looks of anticipation on their faces. We were all hopeful until one woman posed a question.

"What if he passes the test?"

That seemed to dampen the growing excitement. Everyone knew how cool this guy was.

"If it's true what I heard about that machine," someone else said, "a person like him can beat it."

Then a young woman who had visited often but usually kept her thoughts private said, "I had my suspicions about that guy from the very beginning. You're right, he is very cool. I don't know if any of you people have noticed, but he's acting too cool these past three or four days, but not only that, he's become awfully friendly all of a sudden. In the past, that guy never even looked my way. Now when I see him on the road he says 'Hi' and waves at me."

"He won't pass the test," one of the men stated firmly. "I think we got him now, and it's about time. Maybe we can get some kind of life back, and not live in fear of some other child disappearing like Sam."

The afternoon dragged on. Some people were happy, and some were scared. A few weren't showing any signs whatsoever—it seemed these last people were in some kind of daze. I asked a woman what she was thinking.

She shrugged. "I don't know what to think," she said. "I can tell we all have different thoughts on the outcome of this test. Some are happy. But you're not one of them, are you? You're scared of something."

"Well," I said, "in my heart I know Michael is guilty, and the police think so, too. But to find Sam and solve this case, they have to hear what the young man has to say. The lie detector test is the only way we're going get anything out of him, but I think he might beat the machine. If he does, what do we do then? You're right, I'm scared, and I have every right to be. I have a seventeen-year-old daughter and several grandchildren here. I want that scum off the roads."

"My God, Gord," she blurted out, "I've talked to almost every person in this town, and they all think like you do. But me, I can't believe that the young man we're talking about would do such a thing as take someone and kill them, and then hide them! Isn't that what you are saying?"

"Yes," I said, "that's exactly what I am saying."

"Then is there something wrong with me?"

"No, dear," I replied. "There's nothing wrong with you. You are a good person and always have been."

Chapter 8

Millie crawled across the floor to the couch where I was sitting.

"No, no!" she screamed. "He murdered her!" I threw my arms around her as she screamed, "Oh Gord, Oh Gord, he murdered her, he murdered her!"

I met a friend of mine at the town hall, and I asked him if he ever went home.

"Not often," he said. "Home is not like it used to be. My wife and I aren't sleeping, and we haven't been getting along very well for the past week now. I've been saying the same things about this case as everyone else, but when I say how I feel at home, my wife flips out. That poor girl. What's happened to her?"

"You know, Michael agreed to take the lie detector test," I told him, "and we believe he's gone to the police station to do just that." I was surprised to see a look of doubt on his face.

"I wouldn't hold my breath if I were you," my friend replied. "I think I have him figured out. I think we'll be disappointed."

I changed the subject and asked him where he thought Sam's body was. He pointed to the northwest. "Back over those hills somewhere," he said. "If we hadn't had that snowfall, I believe we would have found her body days ago." Then he wiped tears from his eyes, and said, "Those poor people, Millie and George. I know I should go visit them, but I don't have the heart. I don't have a clue what to say to them."

"If you want, you can come with me at about seven," I said. But I knew he wasn't going to show.

I left for my brother's house at quarter past seven. When I arrived, I was greeted by a group of seven or eight strangers. One of them was a member of the RCMP, who sat at the table talking with George. Millie was sitting in a chair by the wood stove, holding one of Sam's teddy bears to her bosom. The look of misery on her face so complete I knew something had happened.

Poor Millie, I thought, *she may not make it through this*.

When she saw me, she immediately burst into tears. "Gord! Oh, Gord!" That had always been the hardest part of being in that house for me. I busied myself making a cup of coffee until the policeman finished questioning George. When they said goodbye and the crowd dispersed, I brought my cup over to the table and sat in the officer's place at the table.

"What happened at the station?" I asked George.

What he said made me slam my fist down on the table. Michael had changed his mind and refused to take the test after all. "That's if he ever had it in his mind to take the test at all," George added bitterly. "I really thought we were going to have something to go on tonight, but now we're no closer to finding Sam than we ever were. Only one thing has come from this. It's made me a hundred per cent sure he is guilty."

When I left George's that night, I didn't stop at the hall as I had done every night for the past two weeks. I went straight home. Ten or so people met me when I walked in, fully expecting me to be the deliverer of good news.

"I'm sorry," I said, "but the news is not what we wanted to hear. He refused to do the test and walked out of the police station."

The same man I had offered to take to George's house was sitting in an armchair. He jumped to his feet.

"Goddamn it," he shouted. "I was afraid of that. Where do we go from here?"

"I really don't know," I replied helplessly.

I could tell my longtime friend was scared. Not scared for himself, because I knew he would like nothing better than to go to Michael Lewis and beat the living shit out of him. He was scared for his family. I told him the only thing I could think of at the moment was to do what we had discussed the day before, to gather a group of men and confront his parents.

Someone gave me a word of caution. "I agree we have to do something," he said, "but it has to be within the law. Remember, Michael is only sixteen years old."

"I know," I said. "I'm more angry tonight than usual, and I'm not thinking straight." At that moment, though, I felt I would have given my blessing to my friend if he decided to go a few rounds with Michael. In fact, I would have liked to do it myself.

"Let's wait two more days," the man who had warned me said, "and see what the police have in mind. Then we'll meet with them and get their thoughts on our plan."

That was two days too long for some, but no one else had any better ideas.

In the end it looked as though holding back on facing Michael's parents was the best thing we could have done. On the eighteenth day, he set out again for Baie Verte with a police escort. This time, we hoped, he would take the test.

"I'll be happy if we don't have to go to his parents that way," one of the men at the town hall said when we learned this.

"You wouldn't have to do it anyway," I replied. "We could get someone else to go in your place."

"Oh, no," he offered, "I'd do my part."

I didn't have much faith in Michael going through with the test, I told him. He had backed out the first time. What made us think he wouldn't refuse the second time?

Around this time, I was told that a man in Gander, in central Newfoundland, had called George and offered to come to Fleur de Lys with his dog and help locate Sam. He must be a decent fellow to come all the way out here and give his services for free, but it didn't excite me to know there was another dog on the way. The police had brought their best dog from Corner Brook to search for Sam only ten hours after she had gone missing, and turned up nothing. Now, after eighteen days, two snow-storms, and people by the hundreds walking over every inch of ground, to bring in one other dog in the hope of finding anything was a waste of time. But George had accepted his offer, and the man was on his way.

The people at headquarters seemed to share George's enthusiasm about the stranger and his dog. Perhaps they knew something I didn't know, I found myself hoping.

"At least there's something new moving for the first time in some days," someone at the hall said to me. "He's gone for the test again, and a new dog is on its way from Gander."

I was having another of my bad days; the strain of all that had happened was taking its toll on me. "Big deal," I replied. "He went in for the test once, and we've already had the best dog out here for two or three days. He didn't find anything that I heard of."

"But they say he's a real good dog," the man told me. "The word is he's found people who have been missing for months. I heard it's a bloodhound."

"I hope something does happen," I said finally. "But I am tired, really tired, and have been for a long time."

He nodded. Everyone was worn out, he told me, and he didn't know how much longer the town could keep going.

Today there seemed to be more police than ever. There also seemed to be more volunteers in Fleur de Lys, from all over the province. Food—cakes, cookies, cooked meats, boilers of soup—was still coming in. Church leaders from all over came each day to pray and to comfort the families. They were all welcome. It didn't matter which religion they were from; we all prayed to the same God.

I left search headquarters and headed home for supper—not that I had been eating well for the past eighteen days. My house was full of people just like every day, friends and strangers alike. I was more than happy to have them for the company. The phone never seemed to stop ringing; family and friends away from home were calling for updates on what was happening. People from all over the province, people I'd never heard of before, were still calling and wanting to know how they could help.

I forgot about the man and his dog. What occupied my thoughts was Michael Lewis. Would he take the test? And even then, would it give us the answers we wanted? My thoughts were interrupted by the phone ringing yet again. I picked up the receiver and answered in an irritable tone of voice.

"The dog handler from Gander would like all the people to be at the church for a meeting at seven o'clock," a man on the other end informed me.

I asked him for details, but the caller said he didn't have time to explain since he had more phone calls to make. It was now ten-past-six and I was eager to hear what this gentleman had to say. Going to the meeting would at least keep me from worrying about the polygraph for a while.

People gathered at the church well before the clock struck seven. We knew there would be a big crowd, as people were glad for anything that broke the monotony of everyday searches that brought them no evidence. No one did a head count, but there had to be four hundred people in attendance, certainly a large crowd for such short notice. I found an empty seat near the front of the church, close to where the visitor was to speak. I needed to hear every word. On the way to the meeting I was told the man and his dog had already gone up in the country to an old cabin the police had checked out a few days before.

When the church had filled to capacity, George stepped up to the microphone and opened the meeting by thanking people for coming and for all their continued support. He then introduced the dog handler as Leonardi Caldi and explained why he had come. He, like many others in Newfoundland, George said, had heard what was taking place in our tiny community. "He called and kindly offered his services. We gladly accepted. I will now let the gentleman explain to you what he does."

Mr. Caldi stepped up to the mike and introduced himself as a tracker from the Atlantic Bloodhound Track and Trail team. He told us he had been doing this kind of work for some time now. He sometimes worked for the law, and he also worked, like he was doing now, for regular citizens.

"My dog Gypsy has found many people," he said, "some missing a day, others a week, and others six months. And she will find Samantha Walsh as well." He paused for what seemed like ages. The silence in the church was deafening; it was as though no one breathed. For eighteen days now, we had been waiting in fear and uncertainty, and now here was a strange man standing in front of us, telling us that he and his dog were going to find Sam. We were taken aback by his confidence that he could get the job done.

Everyone's attention was focused completely on him as he started to speak again. He advised those involved in Sam's disappearance to turn themselves in right now and that, if they did, things would go better for them in court. "If you are a young offender," he said, "you may get seven years. If you want to be stupid, you could and you will get twenty-five years. If you think I don't know what I'm talking about, just pick up the phone and call the Justice Department."

He paused for effect. "There's a young man serving twenty-five years now, and my dog put him there. As I said, Gypsy will find Sam, and when she does, she will backtrack and come to your home. She will go right to your door."

The tracker asked us to bear with him and advise others not present at this meeting that if they looked out their windows and saw a strange man on their land with a dog, it more than likely would be him. "Please don't be alarmed," he said. "I'll be there for one reason only, and that is to find Sam."

He thanked everyone, and the meeting was over. I turned to the fellow next to me. "My God," I said, "he's found her."

"I don't think so," he replied, shaking his head. "I've been here with him all afternoon, and he's found nothing."

"Haven't you been listening?" I asked.

I didn't know what the man and his dog had already done or where they had been, but I was excited about what he had said. It was the first encouraging thing I had heard in the last seventeen days, and now I was hungry for more information.

I learned that when the tracker and his dog arrived in town, they had gone straight to George and Millie's home. They went into Sam's bedroom for a little while, to pick up the scent the dog would follow. Then he took the dog back to the living room where everyone was sitting. The animal approached each person, sniffing them. When the dog had finished, the man said, "She knows that someone who lives here is missing."

He questioned George and Millie regarding their whereabouts during the evening of February 6. They told him about having supper at Sam's grandmother's house and that Sam had left for home at about half-past-six. This, they said, was the last time they had seen her. They also filled him in on eyewitness accounts, the three young boys playing on the ice, and about the young man coming by on his three-wheel ATV and giving Sam a lift.

From there, the tracker and his dog went to the house where Sam had had supper on the sixth. He tied a long rope to his dog and followed some twelve to fifteen feet behind as they covered the short distance to my mother's house. When they reached their destination, he let his dog go to work. She sniffed about the footpath leading from the house to the road, then immediately went on her way, down the very same path Sam must have taken on her way home. She seemed to know where she was going, and I'm very sure her master, who was following behind at the end of the makeshift leash, knew she had caught Sam's scent.

Gypsy passed the spot where Sam had turned off the road and gone to the ice to talk to the three boys. Then, circling back to the road, she passed the bus shelter where Michael claimed he had dropped her off. The dog didn't even look in the shelter's direction. This surprising turn of events raised a few eyebrows. Gypsy continued on past the last home in Fleur de Lys and over the hills on a Ski-Doo trail leading out of town.

Following Mr. Caldi and his dog were Sam's parents Millie and George, and her brother Sandy, along with some of the townspeople who were following on snowmobiles. A couple of times the dog seemed to have lost the scent, but quickly picked it up again. She would leave the road and walk a few yards away, sniff some small area, then return to the trail and continue on its way. They kept going until they came to a cabin about four and a half kilometres northwest of town.

The dog had stopped about thirty paces from the cabin. The tracker bent and talked to her in a language people didn't understand at the time, but later learned was Italian. He informed everyone that his dog was tired, and that they would continue again the next morning. Before leaving, everyone searched the cabin while the man and his dog stayed outside. Inside the cabin, Millie went to a chesterfield and retrieved a hair she thought might belong to Sam.

I was more than a little excited at what had transpired today. After I learned of all that the man and his dog had done, I spoke to Millie and asked her if she believed the dog had found her daughter. I found it very hard to ask Millie this, but I wanted true, honest answers, and I knew I would get honesty from her. I also asked her if something else I had heard was true, that after Gypsy had finished for the day, she had come back to Millie and put its head in her lap.

"Yes," she replied with tears running down her face. "The dog came up to where I was sitting and laid her head in my lap and looked up at me."

She told me she believed in her heart that Gypsy knew she was Sam's mother, and that her daughter's body was close by.

I returned home from the meeting at eight o'clock and was surprised to see only my family members. This was the first time in eighteen days there hadn't been a crowd of at least five strangers milling about. I told my mother everything the tracker had said at the church, and I told the rest of the family I firmly believed the dog had found Sam. I guessed there were two reasons the man had called his dog off. First, family members were nearby, and secondly, he didn't want to disturb any evidence. I said to Clo and Mom the break we had been expecting for so long had finally come. I could hardly wait for morning.

Just then my daughter came in. She talked to her mother for a moment, and I overheard her say, "I wonder how they did at the police station with the lie detector test?"

I jumped. I had been so worked up about what the tracker and his dog had found I had completely forgotten about Michael Lewis and the lie detector test. Had he done the same thing as before, made an appearance only to change his mind and leave the police station? It wouldn't surprise me. From the very start he'd been taunting us and the police.

My thoughts returned to the tracker and his dog, and I smiled. *Take the test or not, Michael. Either way, you'll be in police custody very soon.*

Mom interrupted my thoughts by waving her hand at the northwest hills. "I think Sam is in over those hills and she is dead," she said with a note of finality. She had voiced this opinion several times in the past two weeks but always maintained that Sam's death had been an accident.

I looked across the room to where she sat by the window. As well as my mom, my daughters Helena and Kristie were present, together with my grandson Charles and my wife Clo. I told my mother I agreed with her as far as Sam's location and her being dead. But I told her I thought there had been no accident.

"I think it's something far worse than anything in our wildest dreams, Mom. Something far worse than anything we could imagine ever happening in Fleur de Lys."

She stared at me. "My God, Gord! What are you saying?"

"I think you should prepare yourself for what is to come in the next few days," I said wearily. "Mom," I continued, "there is no easy way to say this. I am pretty sure we are dealing with a murderer."

"Oh, God," she cried, "no, not that!"

I hated telling my eighty-one-year-old mother that her granddaughter in all likelihood had been murdered, but I didn't want her to hear it from someone else. I didn't feel prepared myself, but I felt it had to be done.

That night I was thinking more than usual about what had happened to Sam. I was so lost in my thoughts I didn't hear the people around me talking. The TV was on, people were coming and going, and none of it registered. I didn't even realize I was in a trance until I was brought out of it by a voice coming to me from downstairs.

"Hello," I answered, and asked the visitors to come upstairs. The first to emerge from the basement was Millie. Then followed George, then Steve Barrett, Sam's uncle by marriage. When they reached the top of the stairs, Millie fell to her knees. George slumped onto the arm of Mom's chair, and Steve pulled up a chair next to Mom's.

George was the first to speak. "We have bad news," he said. I held my breath. Michael Lewis, he said, the young man who had been acting so calm and collected in these past eighteen days in the face of constant interrogation, had confessed to killing Sam.

Clo asked if it had been an accident.

Millie crawled across the floor to the couch where I was sitting.

"No, no!" she screamed. "He murdered her!" I threw my arms around her as she screamed, "Oh Gord, Oh Gord, he murdered her, he murdered her!"

I looked at my brother and saw a face I will never forget. I pulled myself together as best I could and tried to talk to them, but found I was speechless. Clo came to Millie and put her arms around her, and they both cried together. George and I stood together in the middle of the room, and I looked into his face.

"I am so sorry," I choked. "I wish there was something I could do for you."

"There is nothing anyone can do now," he sobbed.

Try as I may, I will never find the words to fully describe the scene: the hurt, the anger, the love, the sympathy, the loss, the disbelief—all of this emotion confined to a small room. Before they left my house, George and Millie had calmed somewhat. They said they had already visited Millie's mom and broken the news to her, but that they still had one more home to visit, and one more time to go through all this again. That last home was their own.

My God, I wondered as they were leaving. *How do they keep going?*

I thought of the saying, "God doesn't give you any cross you can't bear," and I couldn't help thinking that their cross was mighty heavy.

Chapter 9

The casket lay twenty feet from the door, over by the far wall. Halfway there a rope had been strung across to prevent people from going too near. I walked as far as the rope with my eyes cast down. It's strange how a person's mind works. Two days after Sam went missing, I was sure she was dead. Now, after all this time, I stood ten feet away from her, not wanting to raise my head and confirm what I had known all along.

The news spread through the town like wildfire. The telephone lines went crazy. Masses of people poured in from nearby communities. My house soon filled with people again, and I was never so glad to have a crowd around me.

I had been talking to Mom again and trying to prepare her for what I thought was coming. I didn't realize
how unprepared I was myself until it met me head-on. I
was so shocked, and for a little while didn't believe what
I had heard, even though I had been talking about this
very possibility for the past two weeks. I never wanted it
to be this way.

Mom was taking it hard. I was worried about her,
afraid that this traumatic news might bring on another
stroke, maybe a fatal one. A number of people from town,
plus two families from Coachman's Cove and two more
families from Baie Verte were staying at my house, and
everyone tried to comfort each other. No one slept that
night. It was one of the longest nights of my life.

The next morning the sun couldn't penetrate the dark
cloud that had had come to stay over Fleur de Lys. After
eighteen agonizing days not knowing if our little girl still
lived and breathed, our worst fears had come true. The
dark cloud had turned black, and I knew it would stay
with me to the end of my days.

I decided I would pay Michael's parents a visit. When
I arrived at their house, his dad was moving around the
house in a daze. He looked busy, but at what I wasn't
sure. I don't think he even knew. I shook his hand and
told him I was sorry for his trouble, and offered to help in
any way I could. His wife was sitting on the chesterfield
with a heavy quilt over her shoulders.

My God, I thought, *she isn't going to make it.* The woman looked like she was dying.

I crossed the room, sat beside her and took her hand in mine. I wanted to say something that might ease her pain a little, but I could think of nothing. No words came to me, so I just held her hand in silence. She squeezed my hand and asked me not to be hard on her son. I stared blankly at her.

Before I left for home, Michael's father phoned George and Millie and asked if it was okay for him and his wife to drop by. "George said they need to do something with the police first," he told his wife as he replaced the receiver, "but we can go over to see them later."

Not long after I got home, my own door opened, and in walked Michael's father again. He sat down, looking worse than he had just a little while ago. "It's shocking," he said, "what has happened." He told me that it was he and his wife who had solved the case.

Michael had confessed to him at his grandfather's house in Baie Verte shortly after he failed the polygraph. He wouldn't speak, so his father urged, "I know you can't talk. Answer me by nodding or shaking your head." He answered all his father's questions like this, never speaking. His dad told me it was the hardest thing he had ever done in his life. He'd lost thirty-five pounds in eighteen days. Clo asked him if he was eating.

"I don't know how to eat."

Later I learned how George and Millie had heard the news. Paul Shelley, our MHA, had been at home waiting for a call from the police. The time for their regular meeting had passed. When Paul called the station to find out what was happening, the police told him to keep George and Millie there. This time the police were going to come to them.

George and Millie had arrived late at the Shelley home. They poured some coffee and went to the basement. Paul told me he could feel something big was about to happen. A few minutes later, the doorbell rang and Paul answered. Two policemen stepped inside, and both of them were crying. The three of them went downstairs and broke the news to George and Millie that Michael Lewis had failed the lie detector test, and that just a little while later he had confessed to killing Sam and burying her body in the snow.

Now the police were back in full force with vehicles of all makes and sizes. They drove to the edge of town, and from there used snowmobiles to haul their equipment to the crime scene. They roped off the trail. No one was permitted to pass that marker as they didn't want anyone to disturb the evidence. What exactly was taking place at the crime scene I don't know. There were rumours that Sam was buried five feet under the snow, and that the police were having trouble finding her because she had been moved. None of these were certain facts. I talked to one of the police officers and tried to find out what was taking place, but he refused to tell me anything.

The next day they told us Sam's body had been found. She'd been buried thirty paces to the rear of the cabin Gypsy had discovered. For the past eighteen days she had lain face down and partially nude in the snow, her shirt and coat pulled up and her pajama bottoms pulled down below her knees.

Earlier they had planned to take Sam's body from the crime scene directly to Baie Verte by chopper. From there, it would be sent to St. John's for an autopsy. But it wasn't until late that evening that the body was taken to town by Ski-Doo, then laid in a police wagon and taken to Baie Verte. Paul Shelley, Millie, George, and Millie's brother Jimmy Lewis received permission to go to the place where Sam had been buried, and not knowing about the change of plans involving the transfer of the body, they went there early in the day. Sam's parents wanted to see where their daughter had been for the last eighteen days.

They drove to the edge of town and stopped when they reached the police cars and vans. An officer took Paul aside. "What in the name of God are you people doing here?" he asked. Paul told him that they had been given permission to visit the place where the body had been found. "I'm sorry," the officer replied nervously.

"Things didn't work out as planned. We didn't get the chopper to transport the body; we're doing it by Ski-Doo. They should be here in a few minutes, so for God's sake, get the parents out of this area."

Paul rushed George and Millie to a dead-end road on the edge of town. Millie asked him to drive to the hilltop and park; she wanted to watch, even if it had to be from a distance. Shortly, she asked him to drive to another place, where the vehicle carrying her baby girl would have to pass. Paul did so. "Everyone in the van was really crying by then," he recalled. "Poor Millie and George were heartbroken." From there they returned to George's home, where many people had gathered to offer their support.

Sam's body remained in St. John's for close to a week. We had no idea it was going to take so long. The days dragged on as we waited for her to come home, and all the time the phones never stopped ringing. People literally from all over the world were calling to offer condolences.

While Sam's body was still at St. John's, preparations were made for her funeral; it would be the biggest funeral this part of the province had ever seen. George requested that there be no more flowers sent—not out of disrespect, but because there wasn't any more space for them. They already had more than they knew what to do with.

Finally, Sam's body was returned to the White Dove Funeral Home in Baie Verte.

Late afternoon the next day, we were told we could visit Sam about seven o'clock in the evening and that the funeral home would be open for family members only. At first we were told that it might be a closed casket. Then we were told this was not so.

The winds had changed and were blowing from the northeast. With this change came freezing rain and, at times, wet snow. We left home at six for the thirty-kilometre drive. Once on the road and in high country, I was glad we did leave early. I've travelled that road many times both day and night, but never did I see the fog so black as on that night. We could see that the rain was turning to ice on the shoulders of the road, but thanks to the salt, the pavement was ice-free. It took an hour to reach the funeral home.

The door to the viewing room was closed and would not be opened until George and Millie came. Most members of our families were there by the time they arrived. I looked at my brother and his wife, and my heart broke for them. All the worry, strain, and sadness from the past twenty-four days was plain to see on their faces. I had never seen anyone hurt as badly as this man and this woman. I hope I never have to see such pain again.

The gentleman in charge of the funeral home, Ed Wilmington, spoke to Sam's parents, then opened the door to the viewing room. George and Millie stepped in and closed the door behind them. The funeral director told us it would be up to them whether anyone else would be permitted to see Sam. After some time, my brother and sister-in-law emerged and said it was okay for us to go in and see their daughter. This time I could not look at them; I moved past them, still not meeting their eyes.

The casket lay twenty feet from the door, over by the far wall. Halfway there a rope had been strung across to prevent people from going too near. I walked as far as the rope with my eyes cast down. It's strange how a person's mind works. Two days after Sam went missing, I was sure she was dead. Now, after all this time, I stood ten feet away from her, not wanting to raise my head and confirm what I had known all along.

Finally, I looked at her, and saw a beautiful child lying in a casket she should not have been in. There was no reason for her to be there, yet there she was, and there wasn't a thing we could do about it. "My God," said a fellow standing next to me. "What a waste of a beautiful young girl." Then, after a pause, he added, "Why?"

I didn't answer. I didn't have any answers, and I knew I never would. I turned and looked around the room. George and Millie were sitting on a sofa, and all the family members had gathered around them. Every person in the funeral home was crying; the sadness in the place was overwhelming. I wondered how George and Millie were feeling right now. For some reason, we always say "we know how you feel," but in reality we don't know, and we never will. It's like a very old saying: You have to walk a mile in their shoes.

I didn't fit in here. I didn't know the right things to say, or when to say the things I would have liked to say. Maybe there are no right words at a time like this. I wanted to leave, but I also wanted to be there at the same time. But I would stay, because my brother and his wife needed all the support they could get.

I went to the kitchen of the funeral home to make myself a coffee. The table was loaded with food, but I didn't feel like eating. I just drained my coffee and returned to the room to join Sam and the family. When I entered I saw that the rope was down, and George was telling people that it was okay to go and view Samantha.

I went to the casket and looked down at a pretty little girl who looked for all the world as if she were sleeping. She wore jeans, a light blue turtleneck sweater, and a pale purple vest with yellow flowers and green leaves. I touched her forehead and hair with my fingertips. Her hair was so soft and silky, with little curls framing her face.

She was beautiful

Before I turned away, I asked God to take good care of my niece. Then I left the room to find a place where I could shed my tears in private.

Chapter 10

*Sam's body arrived in Fleur de Lys at
eleven o'clock in the night. I recalled the
night of February 6, when she left her
grandmother's house for her five-minute
walk home. Now, twenty-four days and
three and a half hours later, my niece
was coming home at last.*

We stayed at the funeral home until ten o'clock.
The weather on the highway worsened, and we arrived
home at eleven. A message was waiting for me to pick
up another of Sam's cousins at the airport in Deer
Lake the following day. For the past three weeks, it
seemed like I was going to the airport every day, but in
truth I didn't mind going. I wanted to do what I could
to help, and besides, two hours gave me some time to
think. It gave me a reason to be away from my

brother's house, and I had to admit I was grateful for that.

When I returned from the airport the following day, I learned that someone had drawn up a schedule in order that one member of the family would be at the funeral home with Sam at all times during the day. It turned out I was scheduled to do the last two hours, between eight and ten. After this, Sam was to be taken home to Fleur de Lys. Throughout that last day, the funeral home remained open for the public, including Sam's friends and classmates. She was visited by countless people who said their tearful goodbyes.

Sam's body arrived in Fleur de Lys at eleven o'clock in the night. I recalled the night of February 6, when she left her grandmother's house for her five-minute walk home. Now, twenty-four days and three and a half hours later, my niece was coming home at last.

George and Millie kept the casket closed in their home, but that didn't stop people from coming to pay their respects. They came all that night and the next day, a steady stream of them. There must have been a thousand or more people who visited the Walsh home in the fifteen hours Sam rested there.

Her grave had been dug in the old cemetery by a large group of men. The old cemetery had been abandoned by a lot of people, except for those who believed loved ones should be laid to rest among their relatives. I believed

Sam's parents wanted her buried there so she could be with her grandfathers, John Walsh and John Lewis.

The road leading northeast to the graveyard was steep and pitted, but the cemetery itself looked out over the waters of White Bay, the distant hills from Englee to St. Anthony to Grey Islands and out to Cape Bauld. The view was breathtaking. To the southwest could be seen most of Fleur de Lys, the town that Sam loved.

On March 2, services were held at St. Theresa's Roman Catholic Church in Fleur de Lys at 7:30 P.M. The church, as expected, was filled to capacity. When I went in, I couldn't find a place to sit. I was escorted to the far end behind the priest and, like many others, shared a chair with a friend. It struck me how the crowd in town had grown in the past month. Since February 6, the police had been using the church to hold their public meetings, and each time there had been a bigger crowd in attendance.

Shortly after I arrived, the service started. Father Edward Brophy presided, and a first and second reader delivered sermons as well. Six or seven people recited poems. Some letters that Sam herself had written were read, as well as many messages from all over the world. Finally, George went to the microphone and said that we could stay there all night, all week, and all next month and still not be able to get through them all. He thanked all the people for coming and for all the help they had given his family.

When the service ended, many people went to George's house and stayed there overnight. That night the temperature dropped a little. It continued to rain, but when the drops touched the ground they turned to ice.

On the morning of the funeral, I was out of bed early. It had been that way for almost a month; sleep wasn't coming easily for anyone at my house. I went to the window for a look at the weather, still hoping it might be a nice day. I wasn't surprised to see what was out there. Wet snow mixed with rain, and everything in sight was covered with ice. The trees were loaded and the branches bent, many broken, many ready to break. I noticed a buildup of ice on the wires.

"My God," I said, "I hope we don't have a power failure." Most ice storms in this area preceded power failures. If that happened, I wondered, how would we feed the people in my house, and the many expected to come that day?

I looked around at the hills surrounding Fleur de Lys. The dark cloud that shadowed our thoughts was thick today. The peaks were hidden in thick black fog.

People arrived early in the day. The house filled very quickly with family and friends. People whom I'd never seen before arrived as well, and all were welcome. Some were from St. John's, some from Corner Brook and Fortune Bay and all the places in between. We made it plain that they were welcome and that they were to serve themselves with the coffee, sandwiches and whatever else they wanted. I jokingly told them that anyone who wanted to was welcome to wash the glasses and mugs as well. After that, things seemed to work out just fine.

One fellow from St. John's said he thought not many people were going to show up to the funeral due to the weather and the icy roads. Later, he had to admit he was wrong. Before noon, every driveway and parking lot was full, and people were parking on the shoulders of the road. I moved my car to make room for others; we managed to squeeze four trucks and cars in there.

On March 1, cable service men strung wires from the church to the two local nightclubs and the town hall. At the same time, business people brought in big screen televisions for those who couldn't get into the church. This way, no one would get to miss out on the service.

Sam's uncles, including myself, were to be pallbearers. I still didn't want to be at my brother's house, but I knew I had no choice. I had been there two different times that day, and each time I met a steady stream of people—men, women, and children—and every one was crying. I knew it would be even worse when we took the casket out. It was always that way at funerals, and this one would be the saddest I had ever attended.

One o'clock came, and it was time for me to be at my brother's house. We would be taking Sam from her home for the last time at two o'clock. When I went outside it was still raining, but I wasn't worried about the weather. I hardly even noticed the cold.

In front of my house a police officer was swinging his arms every which way. For a moment I didn't realize what he was doing. Then I realized he was directing traffic. I looked to my left and there was another police officer doing the same. By this time the roads were lined with vehicles on both sides and a steady stream of vehicles coming and going, looking for parking places. Each building was already filled to capacity, still with some time left before the funeral. This was a large crowd, especially with the weather as bad as it was.

My thoughts returned to what was to take place over the next three hours. I was dreading events: one, when the casket was leaving the home; two, when it was leaving the church; and three, when it was lowered in the ground.

George's house was off the main road and about a hundred feet down a small private lane. Still a long line of people went to and from his house. It amazed me how generous Newfoundlanders can be when one of their neighbours falls on hard times.

I stayed outside until the time came for me to take my place at the casket. The house was so full, I could barely squeeze my way to the room where the pallbearers had gathered. George and Millie just stared at the closed casket, their tears flowing freely. There is crying and then there's crying, but what I heard that afternoon were cries of anguish.

When we got outside and placed Sam in the hearse, I felt relieved to be outside, away from George and Millie, not having to look at their sorrow-filled faces. The fresh air rejuvenated me after the stifling heat of the house.

Besides the hearse were two black trucks provided by the funeral home, one for the family and one for the pallbearers. Once on the way to the church, one of the men asked us if we had ever seen so many people at a funeral before. "No, I haven't," someone answered, "and I don't think I ever will again."

"I can't believe the police officers are directing traffic on the roads of Fleur de Lys," another fellow remarked.

When we arrived, we climbed out of the van and I looked around at the people standing. There were hundreds of them, ranging in age from six months to ninety years old. Once inside the church, we stopped at the back for the placing of the pall. There weren't any seats in this part of the church and people were standing together, packed so tightly they reminded me of sardines in a can. As we moved the casket up the centre aisle, people forced their way in and followed in its wake. Everyone wanted to be in the church.

We sat down in the seats reserved for pallbearers at the front of the church, facing the congregation. From this position, I could hardly believe what I saw. The church was packed to overflowing. There were two priests assisting Father Brophy, and clergy from all other churches in the area. George and Millie sat in the front row on the right, and with them were Sam's brother Sandy, George's mom and Millie's mom. George was holding one of Sam's teddy bears; he was cradling it as though it was Sam herself. The grief and pain had changed his face completely; he was sitting there slumped over like an old man in agony. Millie was under a great deal of sorrow. Her head hung down most of the time, and she was crying. Sandy had something else on his face too, I thought. I could have been wrong, but I thought it was anger. Both the grandmothers were wiping away tears. The past twenty-four days had been a living hell for those five people.

I scanned the congregation. There were a great many strangers, and some I had seen only on TV. Government ministers and other elected officials were in attendance, as well as several from the investigation committee. Some of those present had taken a six- or seven-hour-long drive to get to the funeral.

I hadn't even noticed Mass had started until I heard the opening hymn, *Peace is Flowing Like a River*, sung by the Fleur de Lys Choir. All through the Mass, many of the congregation were in tears, but towards the end the church grew strangely silent. Then Sam's own sweet voice echoed throughout the building, and pictures of her appeared on a screen, first as an infant, then through the thirteen years that followed. Some were of her alone, others of Sam with her brother Sandy, or with her parents, friends and younger cousins.

It was then I prayed I could be a thousand miles away from this church and from all that I had to see and hear. I prayed that I would wake at any moment and find that it had all been a dream. But for some reason, I was forced to keep my eyes open and see the tears running down everyone's cheeks. Then, just when I thought it couldn't get any worse, it happened. We were gathering around the casket to take Sam from the church when Millie became hysterical. She called to her only brother, crying, "Jimmy, oh, Jimmy!" Jimmy came to her and held her in his arms, trying to calm her. Half-blinded by tears, I looked over the congregation again. I could hardly see.

Slowly we walked down the centre aisle with the casket. Mournful cries poured out of every pew as we passed. When we exited into the cool afternoon air, I started to feel better. We placed the casket in the hearse and then got into one of the trucks, waiting for the hearse to move. The driver of the truck, a stranger to me, said, "I've never seen so many people."

"You'd have to have a very thick skin for it not to affect you," another remarked.

I didn't say anything, because I felt the worst was yet to come.

We arrived at the point where the road turned up to the northeast. This road was very steep and, as usual for this time of year, was covered with ice. Two local contractors from Baie Verte, Guy Bailey and Sons and Barkers Construction, had offered their services and equipment to make the roads passable. Barkers Construction owned a tractor suitable for this task, so they did the job, and pretty well. But due to the freezing rain, it was still very slippery.

The casket was transferred from the hearse to a pickup truck, which drove the remaining distance to the gravesite. One other truck also managed to navigate the treacherous road, but most of the people had to walk. The weather had turned very ugly by the time we reached the graveyard, the wind having picked up from the northeast.

Father Brophy had a difficult time reading from his prayer book. He turned his back to the wind and bent over, using his body as a shield to keep the rainwater from the pages. When the prayers were said, I turned away from the grave and the people, including Millie and George. I had seen enough funerals to know what it was like when the casket was lowered into the ground. And today I had heard enough crying and seen enough tears to last me a lifetime.

I walked the short distance to the grave of Sam's grandfather Walsh. After saying the Lord's Prayer, I heard myself say to him, "Pop, did you ever dream such a horrible thing could ever happen in Fleur de Lys?"

I started the lonesome wet walk for home. On my way, the thought came to me that although Sam had been laid to rest, it was far from over. I had heard of many murder cases that had dragged on for as long as four or five years, and I knew that as long as the trial was ongoing, there would be no way for the families to put it behind them and get on with their lives. It was going to be very hard on Millie and George.

Chapter 11

The defense lawyer made it to court this time, and when the judge came in and everyone was seated, he rose and addressed the court. At first I couldn't believe what I was hearing. Michael's lawyer was asking for bail. For a second, there was dead silence; then, one by one, from all over the courtroom, low voices sounded the words, "Oh no!"

The night of March 3 was long and lonesome. Now that Sam had been buried, all of the people who had stayed at my house had returned to their own homes. Now, after almost a month of having the house full of people, there were just the three of us again, Clo, Kristie and myself.

We didn't do much talking, but we all thought the same thing. When one of us did speak, it was about

Sam. I believed it would be that way for a long time to come.

I found myself remembering when Sam was here for supper on Christmas Eve, and thinking about what a pretty girl she had become. *My God,* I thought, *how much can happen in such a short time.* It was strange how the eighteen days we were looking for Sam had seemed like forever while Christmas Eve seventy days ago was like yesterday.

I dreamed about Sam that night, as I had done many nights before. But this time, it was different. Sam was standing with her back turned towards me. She was trying to tell me something, but I couldn't hear what she was saying. I woke up in a cold sweat.

The next day, Saturday, I got out of bed at six, but not to do work of any kind. I just felt better up and around than lying in bed awake. Coffee, something I had recently been drinking by the gallon, seemed to help. After my fourth or fifth mug, I finally went outside. A friend of mine came by and told me he couldn't work, sleep, or eat.

"Anytime I do manage to fall asleep," he said, "I dream about that goddamn young man killing Sam, and I wake up scared and sweating. I don't think I'll ever be the same again."

People were adamant that Michael Lewis be sent to prison rather than a boys' home. The same questions came up over and over again. When will he go to court? What are they waiting for? What's taking so long?

Many were asking whether Michael would be tried as a youth or an adult. Most people were afraid he would be tried as youth, but I had noticed that in the last couple of years some young offenders, sixteen years old and younger, had been charged as adults. I felt sure this would be the case, as the crime had been of a violent nature.

Finally, word came that the young man would appear in court in Baie Verte at 10:00 A.M. Thursday, April 6, two months to the day after he had killed Sam. Some thought it was the wrong day for George and Millie to see him for the first time since he had been arrested and charged. Many didn't want him in the area at all. But others said it was the proper place for him to be put on trial. One of Michael's former friends told me he wanted to look into his eyes once, and then never to see him again. I myself would have liked the whole case to have been heard in Fleur de Lys.

When the day came, many of the town's residents set out early in the morning. They wanted to get a seat in the small courtroom, which could hold no more than sixty people. It was cold that morning, but no one waiting outside the court building seemed to mind. At a quarter to ten, the doors were opened and we filed inside and found ourselves seats. The courtroom soon filled to overflowing.

A police officer held up his hand to get everyone's attention. "When the judge comes in," he said, "he will ask the ones who are standing to leave. Only those who are seated will be allowed to stay."

There was a murmur of disappointment, but those left standing exited the room obediently. Outside, a crowd from all the nearby towns had gathered and was steadily growing. Many were students of Sam's age, some younger.

Finally, the prisoner entered in handcuffs and was escorted to a chair in front of the judge's bench. George, Millie and myself sat in the front row, on Michael's right. Where George sat he could very easily lay his hand on the young man's left shoulder. At the sight of the young criminal, a kind of chill rushed through me. *I am in a room,* my thoughts raced, *where not four feet in front of me is the man who murdered my niece and hid her body from the world for eighteen days.* At that moment I wanted so badly to put that piece of shit away.

But then I thought of my brother. *My God, what must be in his mind! It was his baby that this guy murdered.* I found myself praying for George to keep his cool. He wasn't one to lose control, not like me; I was the hotheaded one among the men in our family. I often said how I'd like to be like George, as he could handle anything. But, then, we had never been in a circumstance such as this, and I didn't know if he could handle it.

The first two or three minutes of waiting were the scariest for me. But then Judge Luther called the court to order. The Crown's lawyer stood right away and told the court that the lawyer for the accused could not be there that day and wanted to set a date for sometime in August. The judge said he thought that was too long and set it for May 18 instead.

We left the courtroom. Once outside, people started to voice their opinions. "We shouldn't fuck with him," said a man I didn't know. "We all know he did it; lock him up and throw away the key." Someone else mumbled that this could all take two or three years.

I started for home, feeling sad that more had not been done. We had waited two whole months and all that had happened was a change of date. One of the men riding with me said, "I always wondered why the court system had such a backlog of cases, and now I know. I don't know too much about murder trials, but I will learn, because I'm going to follow this one to the end."

The days dragged on between then and the eighteenth of May. Once more a large crowd, not as big as on April 6, attended. This time the students had not been excused from class. Still, there were some who refused to obey the teachers and showed up at the court building anyway.

The courtroom was full. Everything looked the same. George and Millie sat in the exact same seats as before.

And when they brought Michael in they seated him in the same place he had sat back in April.

The defense lawyer made it to court this time, and when the judge came in and everyone was seated, he rose and addressed the court. At first I couldn't believe what I was hearing. Michael's lawyer was asking for bail. For a second, there was dead silence; then, one by one, from all over the courtroom, low voices sounded the words, "Oh no!"

I looked around the room and eyed the mothers and fathers of Fleur de Lys. I knew most of them; some of them had children Sam's age. They seemed to have just frozen in their seats, and there was a look in their eyes I couldn't mistake for anything other than fear.

Here we were, knowing what we knew, and I was sure the defense lawyer knew it as well. He might have had children or grandchildren of his own. And yet he stood before the people of Newfoundland, and those of Canada, asking that a man who had done all of these things be released onto the streets.

I personally didn't think he would make bail, but it was a worry for me. If for some crazy reason he got out, he would be living among people somewhere in this world, and he didn't deserve that freedom anymore.

The people in this little town were terrified at the thought of Michael Lewis getting out of jail. His parents were satisfied to take responsibility for him if he did make bail, but that was far from reassuring. If they couldn't control their son before he killed Sam and before he confessed, what made them think they could control him now? Most people were sure they were not capable of keeping the young man under control, and that he would go where he wanted, when he wanted, and that included coming back to Fleur de Lys. I'm sure there were a few, however, who deep down had big plans for this monster should he make bail.

The defense and the Crown lawyers talked for a while and agreed on a bail hearing. The judge granted the application, and a date was set for the hearing. It was to start 9.30 A.M. on June 22 at the Springdale courthouse.

Early morning on June 22, many Fleur de Lys residents were on their way to Springdale, a one-and-a-half-hour drive. This time people carried signs and placards reading REMEMBER SAM, JUSTICE FOR SAM, and so on. These were placed in front of the courthouse in plain view of the public. Signs and pictures of Sam were also hung between trees across the road from the courthouse. Women and children wore "sandwich" signs around their fronts and backs. People were willing to go anywhere and do anything to keep this young man behind bars.

It seemed the black cloud that had come over our little town on February 6 was darkening and thickening by the day. Some mothers were visibly shaken; they had convinced themselves that Michael Lewis would make bail and would be free to walk the streets. They weren't scared only for their children, but also for themselves.

We had more public support this time. Less than two weeks before the court date, people had racked their brains to come up with something that might help keep the young man from getting bail. Someone came up with the idea of a petition. Although there was little time to get it out to where people could sign it, we were not surprised at the vast number of signatures we did get, somewhere between twelve and thirteen thousand. One thing that surprised me was that three or four people wouldn't sign. The petition was sent to the Minister of Justice, Kelvin Parsons, at St. John's.

The courtroom in Springdale was very small, with enough seating for perhaps twenty-four people. Before the proceedings started, I was asked to leave the room. As I had already given a statement, it was possible I might be called to the stand sometime during the trial. So I went outside before Judge Reid came in, and waited all day with many other people from Fleur de Lys and Springdale.

About an hour and a half after court started, a man and wife came out and told me they were going home because they couldn't hear anything. The air conditioner behind them had been too loud, and muffled the voices of the court officials and witnesses. They said it had been turned off for a while, but then the judge had ordered it back on.

I learned afterwards who had been on the stand that day. The first one up was Michael's mother. Next had been his father, and then a man from the Department of Education. Next up had been the young man himself, then P.W.C. Paddy McNeil, Corporal, B Division Serious Crime Unit West. The last up for the day had been Sam's mom, Millie Walsh.

The following day, the Crown attorney, Linda Moore, planned on calling many witnesses, some of them boys ranging in age from thirteen to fifteen. We were expecting a long day. Court was to start at nine-thirty, but before the time came, we could see something was happening. The police and the Crown lawyer were talking to some of the young boys, when the defense lawyer came out and signalled for the police and the Crown lawyer to join him. They talked in private for a while, then returned to court. Half an hour later, they emerged and told us that the defense had withdrawn its application for bail.

At first glance it seemed the people from Fleur de Lys were not happy to hear this. Many were crying. But on closer inspection, it could be seen that they were crying and laughing at the same time. Sam's parents were very pleased with the decision. When we arrived home that day, we had a reason to smile at last—though it was early in the game, justice had won a small victory that day. There came an opening in the black cloud over Fleur de Lys that, though small, was still a glimmer of light.

The next court date would be a transfer hearing scheduled for September 25 in Grand Falls-Windsor. This was our next big hurdle, that Michael Lewis might be tried as a young offender. If that happened, he would get a slap on the wrist and be back on the street in no time. When you hear in the news of some light sentence being handed down for a person who had killed their young child or intentionally shot another person, it makes you wonder about our justice system. The three months we carried this worry with us were very slow in passing.

This time I was told I was not going to be called to the stand, so I could sit in the courtroom for the rest of the hearing and the rest of the trial.

On September 25, the defense was first to call their witnesses before Judge Hyslop. The first was a doctor from St. John's. Again, the mike was turned off. The judge was very soft-spoken, and the lawyer even more so, and it was impossible to hear what was being said. The doctor was the only one on the stand that day.

The next day, the defense called a female doctor from St. John's, and it was the same. We were still unable to hear, and I was getting pissed off. I let it be known in the hall outside the courtroom that I wanted an explanation why the mike had not been turned on.

After a short recess, the judge mentioned that someone had complained about not being able to hear, and he agreed to have the mikes turned on. "But," he warned, "if they interfere with me or the counsel, I will have them turned off again. It is my right to do so if I wish." For the remainder of the afternoon, which was only about half an hour, everything was loud and clear.

The next morning when the judge called court to order, there was an echo on the microphone system. Right away he ordered the system turned off, and we were back where we started, unable to hear anything. I believed that for some reason they didn't want the people in the courtroom to hear what was being said. Next up was a child social worker from Baie Verte. Then there followed a superintendent of jails and correction facilities.

On September 27, the defense called Michael's mother to the stand. "This will be my last witness for this hearing," the defense lawyer said to the judge. He asked her a few questions, most of which we could hear.

Then it was the Crown's turn to question the woman. "I guess this is a situation you never thought you'd be in," the Crown attorney began.

"Yes," she agreed.

After talking in this vein for a while, the lawyer said, "I'm going to put a scenario before you." When he resumed, it seemed like was he was reading from something. But he didn't get very far before the defense lawyer jumped to his feet and objected. He told the court he had been handed the statement the Crown was reading from only five minutes before court had started that morning. The information had not been disclosed properly, therefore he had not had ample time to study it. The judge and lawyers had a conference among themselves.

We were told that court was postponed and would resume again on October 10.

October 10 came, and Michael's mother was on the stand again. The Crown completed its cross-examination, then the defense asked for a postponement until the next day. The next day we sat for only five minutes before the hearing was put off again, this time until the sixteenth.

Clo and I decided to spend the night with my nephew in Glenwood the day before the hearing. By staying overnight and travelling to court the following morning, we would save three hours' driving time. We arrived at the courthouse in Grand Falls at 9:30, half an hour before court was to start. But I had been through this enough times now to know that it never started on time. If they said ten o'clock, it was a safe bet the proceedings would not begin until ten-thirty or eleven. It was no different this morning. Eventually the Crown arrived, and a little while later the defense showed up. The judge was the last to show.

There had been all kinds of rumours flying before we got into the courtroom that morning. The one that made the most sense to me was that the defense wanted a plea bargain: second-degree murder in adult court. When the judge began speaking, his voice was even lower than before. Within ten minutes, court was over and we were outside again. It was only then I heard that the hearing was to be moved to St. John's and would resume on November 3. I didn't ask any questions, because no one seemed to had heard exactly what had been said.

My wife and I started debating whether we should go to one of the restaurants for lunch or head straight home. At that moment, Sam's mother came out from the building. She was crying again today. Some days were worse than others, and this was a bad one.

"Millie is having a hard time," Clo told me. "She's taking it harder with each passing day and each court appearance."

On the way home that afternoon, we talked about Sam and why things like this happened, and why of all places they should happen in Fleur de Lys, our small town of one big family. We talked about what Sam might have become—maybe a doctor, a lawyer, a mom and even grandmother. Whatever her dreams had been, they had come to an end when that young man choked the life from her young body back in February. We would never see, hear or touch Sam ever again.

It was at times like this I got really mad at the guy and at this cruel world in which we live. It would be over two weeks until the trial could resume in St. John's. For me it would be a very long two weeks indeed. If only I could get my mind on something else, something to do to pass the time. But I'd tried that before and had always drawn a blank.

I had a little workshop in which I used to spend many hours working with wood. I used to enjoy my time in there very much. But since the night Sam disappeared, I hadn't been able to do anything in there. I couldn't focus on anything; my mind was always on Sam and what had happened to her. Time used to slip away so fast when I worked at my little carpenter shop. But that was in the past now.

Chapter 12

Right then, I lost what control I had. He must have seen something in my eyes, because he stopped in mid-stride. All those months of torture and misery stored inside me were now ready to erupt. I turned to face him fully and yelled, "Fuck you! You call it fair for the likes of that to murder a thirteen-year-old girl and be locked up for a lousy seven years? You call that fair?"

I left home at 7:00 A.M. on November 2 for the long drive to St. John's. With good weather and very few hold-ups, I covered the distance in seven hours. By the time I arrived in town, the sky had turned black with fog. I stayed at my nephew's house that night, and the next morning at ten o'clock I was sitting in the courtroom again.

The police officer from Baie Verte who had told me court would only take about two minutes knew what he was talking about. He'd described it like this: "Walk in, sit down, get up, walk out." And that was how it happened. The judge brought the court to order, then the defense stood and said his client was withdrawing his application for transfer. Very quickly, a date was set for November 9 in Corner Brook, and that was that.

On the way home, we talked for hours about the court dates, and why they had taken place all across the province. We wondered why the trial had not been held each and every time in nearby Baie Verte. To me it seemed ridiculous that we had to make fifteen-hour round trips just to sit in court for two or three minutes. Michael had been charged in Corner Brook, the second phase had been in Baie Verte, the next one in Springdale, then in Grand Falls, then St. John's, and now the trial was finally going back to Corner Brook.

The weather continued its miserable descent through November 8, the day before court. Rain, drizzle, lots of fog, and the forecast was calling for the same the next day. We left home for Corner Brook and booked ourselves into a hotel for that night and the next.

Corporal Paddy McNeill asked us to be at the court-room for 9:00 A.M. the next day, as he was expecting a crowd. He told us he would like to get the families in first, well before court started at ten. He was right about the crowd; the courtroom itself was packed solid, and the room outside overflowing. Judge Welsh at least agreed to leave the double doors between the rooms open, and to supply as many chairs as could be found.

Court was a little late starting, but when the time came, the prisoner appeared at the courtroom door escorted by two guards; one male, one female. This time he was in chains, both wrists and ankles, which were removed before he entered the courtroom. I looked for some sign of remorse in his face, but it was useless. There was nothing there to see. He kept his eyes downcast, not looking at anyone directly. He hadn't changed much these last few months. He could have been slightly taller than last I'd seen him and maybe a few pounds heavier, but the stony expression on his face remained as always.

Clo and I were sitting closer to Michael than anyone in the courtroom. Ninety per cent of the time I kept my eyes on him, wondering how anyone could do to a person what he had done to Sam. In the news that night, one of the reporters said he looked like he had shed a tear. But I knew this wasn't so. Michael sat the whole time with his head hanging down. Two or three times, he rubbed his eyes with his knuckles, but there were no tears. Since February 6, I had seen a lot of crying, and that wasn't it.

The Crown read an excerpt from the autopsy report and then from the prisoner's statement. All the while I kept my eyes on the young man who had taken Samantha Walsh from her parents and the town that loved her. Perhaps I was looking at him too much, as I noticed the two guards started watching me. I guessed they thought I would do something. I didn't, but, oh, I wanted to.

The Crown finished reading, and there was a short recess. After the break, Sam's father took the stand and read his impact statement. While he was walking to the stand, Michael's father left the courtroom. George got through two lines before breaking down.

"He won't be able to do it," I remember saying to my wife.

He read, cried, stopped, read and cried again. I thought back to the night when George and Millie came to my home to tell us the news that Michael had confessed to murdering Sam. I thought of the times I was at his house after Sam went missing. I thought of the funeral, and of Sam's young voice singing her favorite song, *Saltwater Joys*. I remembered how at the gravesite I had thought that the hardest and saddest time was over for me; it had never entered my mind that more was to come that would be just as sad. I knew that at the trial George would have to go to the stand as well as Millie, but I hadn't expected it to be this hard.

I heard someone say George was crying like a baby. "No," I said, "he is crying like a grown man for his baby."

I was very angry, and for the first time in my life I really wanted to hurt someone. While my brother was on the stand crying and talking about his baby girl, there was a feeling in my stomach the likes of which I had never experienced before. *My God,* I thought, *will this ever end?* But the answer came as fast as the question had. The answer was no, at least not for me. Everyone from Fleur de Lys felt a dark cloud's presence, but the cloud for me was cold and black.

Millie was the next to take the stand, and she didn't have it any easier. I looked across the room at the Lewis family, the father having returned after George left the stand. The mother looked sad, sick, and pitiful. Agony was written plainly on her face. The father also looked like he'd seen better days. He looked like someone whose heart had been ripped from his body.

My attention returned to Sam's mom on the stand. At the end of the statement, she started to lose control and became hysterical. The judge asked for a person to come forward and help her.

Next on the stand was one of Millie's sisters. She explained how the murder and Sam's disappearance had impacted her family. When she finished and returned to her seat, there was a five-minute recess. The judge reminded everyone it was supposed to be five minutes, not fifteen like the previous break. But hardly anyone left the room; some just stood for a little while to ease their backsides from sitting for so long.

When the session recommenced, the defense restated its plea of second-degree murder. And with that, the judge ordered Michael Lewis to stand. "I find you," her voice carried over the crowd, "guilty of second-degree murder." There would be another five-minute recess, she said, after which sentencing would begin.

Judge Welsh returned. She instructed Michael to stand again. In her soft voice, she said that what he had done was commit a brutal murder. "You are sentenced to life without chance of parole for seven years," she finished.

We knew before we went to court that day that if Michael pleaded guilty to second-degree murder the sentence could come under seven years, but not over. I was a little relieved by the sentence the judge had given him, though not happy. I knew that what it would take for me to be happy—life without parole, life for as long as he was breathing—would never happen.

When we came out of court, I spoke with a few friends who were seated in the room outside. Before going on to the ground floor, a man whom I had never seen before pushed himself from the wall and came directly for me.

"What do you think of it now?" he asked, looking me in the eye.

I was surprised.

"Think of what?"

"The sentence," he said.

"Not much," I answered, "but the judge gave him all she could, and that will have to do."

"Seven years," he answered, not lowering his gaze. "He has one served, so he'll be out in six. A fair sentence, I'd say."

Right then, I lost what control I had. He must have seen something in my eyes, because he stopped in mid-stride. All those months of torture and misery stored inside me were now ready to erupt. I turned to face him fully and yelled, "Fuck you! You call it fair for the likes of that to murder a thirteen-year-old girl and be locked up for a lousy seven years? You call that fair?"

For the second time that day, I wanted to hurt someone, this time a complete stranger.

"Everyone deserves a second chance," he argued.

"Not a fucking murderer," I stated firmly. "He doesn't deserve to live."

I turned my back on him. I didn't have anything else to say.

Someone said on the ride home, "Well, court is over."

I didn't say anything. I was thinking there was a slight chance it might not be. Michael Lewis had thirty days in which he could appeal the sentence, though I was willing to bet he wouldn't. There were still witnesses I was sure he didn't want to come forward should the trial continue.

Epilogue

On January 10, 2001, while talking with my brother George, I was very surprised to learn that there was going to be another court hearing for the young man who had killed Sam.

"What for?" I asked.

He told me he wasn't sure himself, but believed it was being held to make a decision on where to send him to serve out his sentence. This surprised me even more; all the people I had talked to seemed to think Michael Lewis would automatically go to an adult prison. After all, he had pleaded guilty to second-degree murder as an adult and been sentenced in an adult court.

I am learning more each day about our stupid justice system, I thought. *With each new court appearance the whole thing seems more and more pointless.*

I had attended all the court hearings since this tragic ordeal began, and I would attend this one in Corner

Brook, even if I had to walk the two hundred and sixty kilometres. I felt this one was going to prove to me what I already suspected about our justice system and the Young Offenders Act. I had heard after the last court session that Michael would be staying at the Youth Centre in Whitbourne until he had finished his education.

The court was to be held at 10:00 A.M. on January 17 and continue over to the next day. That meant we were to leave our homes early in the morning, knowing that the roads from Fleur de Lys to Baie Verte would be snow-covered and icy. We had no idea what the Trans Canada Highway would be like. My grandson, Charles Walsh, would be with us the first morning as he was one of Sam's best friends and felt he should be there. We needed to bring him home before the second day, however, because he had school.

The morning of January 17 was a fine day—cold, but sunny with cloudy periods. The road from Baie Verte to Corner Brook was clear and our journey swift. When I entered the courtroom, I saw some folks from Fleur de Lys who had made the trip to support George and Millie. Sam's parents hadn't arrived yet, and neither had the parents of the convicted murderer. I recognized one of the police officers, Sgt. Bruce Whillans from Baie Verte.

Before going in the courtroom, a man who seemed to be a worker there asked me what I thought would happen today.

"I don't know," I answered.

"You can expect anything," he said. "The justice system is too soft on these guys, and getting softer every day."

Soon, Sam's parents arrived and sat to my left, and a few minutes later, Michael Lewis's parents and his two sisters appeared. Following them were Millie's brother and his wife.

The side door opened and Michael walked in without any cuffs or chains. By the look of him, someone who didn't know better might think he was up on a charge of killing a moose, or crossing the road on a snowmobile. Following him at a distance of about twelve feet was an officer and a man in plain clothes, a guard. Michael walked to the box and sat down nine or ten feet to my right. He still hadn't changed. I don't claim to be a mind reader, but he looked like someone who knew what was coming. He looked bored.

"All rise."

The judge walked behind the bench and spoke to the Crown lawyer, Mr. Cardwell, who then addressed the court for forty-five minutes. Mr. Cardwell spoke very quietly and I didn't get all that he said, except that he did not think the Youth Centre was the right place for the young man.

Then the defense lawyer got up. He started to talk about the young man's age and how well he was doing and what a good boy he was. He was painting a pretty picture of the murderer sitting behind him. I could tell the judge was buying everything he was saying. When the defense finished, I wondered how many coats it would take to make a good guy out of Michael Lewis.

The judge must have agreed with everything the defense lawyer had argued. She said the young man would be placed in the Youth Centre at Whitbourne. I wondered how many children these people had to lose before they came to their senses. What would it take, I thought, for them to do the right thing and put these criminals away for life? A life sentence, to me, is not twenty-five years. Life means being being locked up until the day you die.

The black cloud that had settled over Fleur de Lys on February 6 opened just a little, first when they decided to cancel the bail hearing, again when they withdrew the application for transfer back to juvenile court, and once more when Michael Lewis was sentenced to life with a minimum of seven years before parole.

But I believe the cloud will stay for a very long time. I've spoken to people from the very young to the very old who have been affected by this tragedy. They say they will always be changed by the murder of young Samantha Walsh. Father Edward Brophy said it best when at Sam's funeral Mass he asked, "Will the flowers ever grow again in Fleur de Lys?"

Sam's grandmothers are both getting on in years. Both have been devastated by Sam's murder and will remain so for the rest of their lives. I have a four-year-old granddaughter, Kira, who is always talking about Sammy and asking why the young man killed her. I heard her ask a question of her grandmother one day.

"Nan, if Sammy was his friend, and he was Sammy's friend, how come he killed her?"

Kira expected an answer, but there was none. No one has the answer. I know that my granddaughter and many other children in the province of Newfoundland and Labrador will be deeply affected by what happened in Fleur de Lys on that Sunday night, February 6, 2000. They will be affected for a very long time to come. And that is why I feel the black cloud will stay with us for a long, long time.

I know that, for me, the black cloud is my own life sentence.

A Note of Thanks
On Behalf of Sam's Family

We would like to thank everyone personally who sent cards, letters, emails, phone calls, and for your prayers.

Thanks to those who joined in the search whether you were from Fleur de Lys or from far away. Without your help the seach would have been impossible or taken years to complete.

Just to name a few groups and individuals:

The police for a job well done.

Eddie Wimbleton and family from White Dove Funeral Home for their excellent services.

Search and Rescue: Especially the divers who risked their lives in the frigid waters.

Leonardo Caldi and his dog Gypsy.

Doctors, nurses and counsellors.

All the clergy and churches.

Everyone who cooked food and personally delivered it to Fleur de Lys.

All the people for freely using their machines in the search.

Local contractors: Bailey's, and Barker's, for the use of their machinery whenever it was needed.

The many hundreds of people who paid their last respects at the funeral home and at Sam's home.

To all the people who came from so far away in extremely poor driving conditions to be with Sam's family and relatives during her funeral service.

The Red Cross.

To the people of Fleur de Lys as well as those in nearby communities who have small kids, teenage boys, teenage girls, who went through the horrendous ordeal for those eighteen days, but still managed to do what was expected and requested of them.

For all this, we thank you so very, very much.

Sam was buried on a Friday afternoon.

Two days later, on Sunday, Fleur de Lys experienced a severe power outage that affected every home. Coupled with the late events, everyone was edgy as they sat in their houses in the cold. In the afternoon, there was a knock on our door, and when I answered, there were two ladies standing outside. One of them asked how many were in the house. She then explained that they were delivering meals, cold-cuts for every man, woman and child in Fleur de Lys.

These people had come from Middle Arm, about an hour's drive away. Knowing the emotional and physical state we were in, this little community had gotten together and prepared meals for us to show how much they cared for us in our time of sorrow. There were many tear-filled eyes in Fleur de Lys that day.

This thoughtfulness and generosity reminded us that amongst evil, good intentions and simple, noble acts will triumph. On behalf of Fleur de Lys I would like to thank the people of Middle Arm, Green Bay for thinking of us and looking after us on that day.

Gordon Walsh

Thanks to Gordon

Our dear and only child, our daughter known fondly as Sam to many, Sammie to her Daddy, and Samantha to her Mom, is dead. Gone from this earth forever. Sammie didn't die. She was murdered. Gone forever, gone somewhere, but where? This is the reality of each waking moment for her mom and dad.

Neither of us could find the strength to write about this terrible and unfortunate tragedy, and words for us seem trite in describing what follows when your child is murdered, stripped from your life. However, we are indebted to Gordon Walsh, Samantha's uncle, for having the strength, perseverance, and determination to scribe the events of what a community was experiencing and continued to experience for the duration of Sam's disappearance, the unveiling of an ugly truth, and the aftermath of this horrendous ordeal.

Thank you, Gordon, and may your readers have a truer understanding of what did occur. It is with hope that it will be realized just what the world will have to deal with if parole is granted to Michael John Victor Lewis.

We would like to take this opportunity to express our sincere love and gratitude to the people of Canada, and, in fact, globally for each gesture of love, kindness and understanding bestowed upon us during our tragedy. It is with special warmth we express our gratitude to our fellow Newfoundlanders and Labradorians. We know that you cried with us, and we continue to find strength from your love and sincerity. It will be forever in our memory and hearts. More so, the little children, who expressed their care in script or drawings. We cherish each individual piece, and still find comfort in these messages. To thousands of teenagers, a special thank you, and may your lives be touched by Sammie.

Samantha loved life and all it had to offer, including her friends and her love of song and music. May you spread Sammie's love for life by living yours responsibly and honestly, and appreciate all the saltwater joys in your lives.

George and Millie Walsh
Fleur de Lys

Gordon Walsh is the second oldest in a family of eleven children born to John and Bertha Lewis Walsh of Fleur de Lys. He fished with his father out of Fleur de Lys before working in the lumber camps for Bowaters of Corner Brook. He also fished on the Labrador for two years.

. He is married to the former Clotilda Quigley, and they have four daughters and one son. After ten years as a heavy equipment operator in the Baie Verte asbestos mine, the author returned to fishing for ten years. He was later employed with the town council of Fleur de Lys until retiring for health reasons.

Samantha Bertha Walsh, the subject of this book, is his niece.